Into the C

A look at Tiny Core Linux

Lauri Kasanen et al

Into the Core: A look at Tiny Core Linux

Lauri Kasanen et al

Publication date 2013

Copyright © 2013 Lauri Kasanen

First edition

ISBN 978-952-93-3391-2

The ISBN is only valid for the printed edition. The PDF is not considered a published work in the sense that it would need an ISBN.

Dedication & thanks

This book wouldn't be possible without Robert Shingledecker, without whom Tiny Core itself wouldn't exist.

I would like to thank Andyj, Coreplayer2 and Richard A. Rost for helpful comments and suggestions.

Chapter contributors to this book, in alphabetical order:

* Luiz Fernando Estevarengo

Table of Contents

Preface

This book mainly targets those with some familiarity with Linux, with no fear of the command line. A spirit of tinkering is advised, but not necessary.

Reading the chapters in order is not necessary, so feel free to jump to the interesting parts directly.

The book is current for the latest stable 4.x for the x86 architecture, 4.7.7 at the time of writing, though many of the principles apply to other versions and architecture ports.

1. Conventions

 This is a note.

 This is a tip.

 This is a warning.

Shell script looks like this:

```
$ echo Code to be typed into an unprivileged shell.
# This is a comment.
$ echo This is a long line extended \
  into many lines. The backslash can be written \
  as is, the shell will understand it.
```

Part I. Intro & basic use

Chapter 1. Core concepts

 This chapter is an edited version of the one available on our web page.

On behalf of the Tiny Core Team, welcome. Please take the time to read this document and understand the philosophies behind Tiny Core.

One quick user beware: Tiny Core is not a turn-key operating system. At least initially, almost all users will require internet access to the online repository.

1.1. Philosophies

As a quick summary, Tiny Core loads itself into RAM from storage, then mounts applications on storage, or installs applications to RAM from storage. An extension is said to be *loaded* or *installed* regardless of the method used (mount vs. copy to RAM).

Tiny Core is different because users are not encouraged to perform a *traditional*, hard-drive installation of the operating system. Sure, a hard drive installation is possible, but Tiny Core is designed to run from a RAM copy created at boot time. Besides being fast, this protects system files from changes and ensures a pristine system on every reboot. Easy, fast, and simple renew-ability and stability are principle goals of Tiny Core.

If this sounds similar to what many live CDs do, the techniques are indeed similar and shared.

1.2. Frugal install

Frugal is the typical installation method for Tiny Core. That is, it is not a traditional hard drive installation, which we call "scatter mode", because all the files of the system are scattered all about the disk. With frugal, you basically have the system in two files, **vmlinuz** and **core.gz**, whose location is specified by the boot loader.

Any user files and extensions are stored outside the base OS.

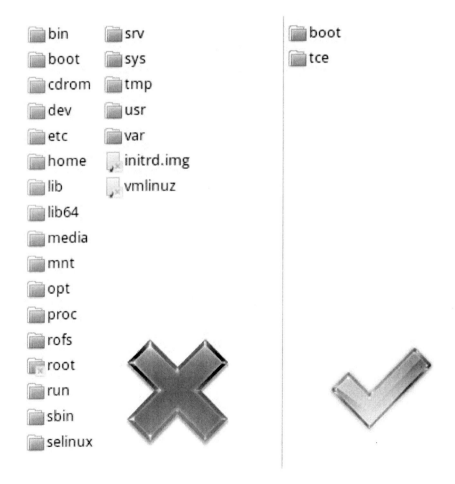

1.3. Boot codes

Depending upon how Tiny Core is installed (GRUB, LILO, CD, USB stick ...), users have the option to use boot codes on each reboot (CD, etc), or to store those codes in a boot configuration file (GRUB, LILO, etc.).

Boot codes (boot arguments) affect how Tiny Core operates by defining options at boot-time. There are lots of boot codes. To view all the available options, peruse the boot code lists by pressing F2, F3 or F4 at the CD boot prompt.

The boot code **base** is notable. Use **base** to simulate the default mode and skip all application extension installing or mounting. This is a useful tool for troubleshooting, extension building, upgrading ... and just checking out how fast Tiny Core can boot on your hardware.

1.4. USB and other external storage devices

Tiny Core can be instructed to search for data on external devices at boot time: a USB pen drive, compact flash, or other portable media. This need not be the boot media; in fact, for example it is common to store user data on a hard disk, while booting from cd or USB.

Sometimes, hardware doesn't wake up fast enough for Tiny Core's boot sequence. If the hardware doesn't wake up in time, Tiny Core will move on and finish booting without that data.

If you store data on external/slow media, it may be necessary to use the boot code **waitusb=5** or similar. This pauses the boot process for five seconds, waiting for slow devices to register with the system bus.

1.5. Dependency checking and downloading

Tiny Core makes getting applications as easy as possible. The Apps tool provides application details from individual .info files - this is enlightening reading material when choosing applications. Always read the .info files, and re-read them before upgrading to catch changes and concerns.

Dependencies are the pieces (other applications, libraries) required for an application. In short, the Tiny Core Apps tool will take care of downloading and checking dependencies for you.

1.6. Modes of operation

The modes of operation mix up how Tiny Core loads, mounts, and installs at boot time (see philosophies, above, if you want to clarify what those three things mean here). Tiny Core has three main modes:

- Default mode: cloud/internet

- Mount mode: TCZ/install

- Copy mode: TCZ/install + copy2fs.flg/lst

Again, some may say there is a "Traditional mode: install to a hard drive", but that's not really a mode at all. If you want to do it, go right ahead. It's just not one of the original goals of the project, so expect to keep both pieces if it breaks.

1.7. The default mode: cloud/internet

By default, Tiny Core Linux operates like a cloud/internet client. In default mode:

Tiny Core boots entirely into RAM. Users run the Apps tool to browse the repository and download applications. Application Extensions (downloaded applications) last only for the current session. Tiny Core just uses as much RAM as possible.

Since Cloud/Internet Mode operates out of RAM, it runs fast. Cloud/Internet Mode is nomadic and quick-booting. Application extensions are lost on reboot, but only the system files have to be restored. If you would like applications stored locally and set up on each reboot, then consider the mount and copy modes.

1.8. Mount mode

This is the most widely used and recommended method for using Tiny Core.

Applications are stored locally in a directory named **tce** on a persistent store, e.g. a supported disk partition (ext2, ext3, ext4, vfat). Applications are optionally mounted on reboot (see onboot.lst in forum and wiki). Mounting applications saves RAM for other uses.

Unless specified with a boot code of **tce=xdyz** Tiny Core will search all drives on the computer and use the first /tce directory it finds for storing/loading extensions.

Tiny Core uses the Apps tool to place application extensions in this tce/ directory and to flag them as either "OnBoot" (mount at boot) or "On Demand" (do not mount at boot, but create a special menu section for easy access and display an icon if available).

```
tce/
`-- optional/
    |-- firefox.tcz
    |-- opera.tcz
    `-- thunderbird.tcz
```

1.9. Copy mode

The copy mode is a modification of the mount mode.

Selected application extensions are copied into RAM instead of mounted. Applications can be RAM-loaded in bulk (copy2fs.flg), selectively loaded into RAM (copy2fs.lst), or mounted. The Apps program tracks installation/loading options (bulk copy, selective copy, etc). Boot times are longer, since copying to RAM takes more time than mounting, but runtime speed, especially first start, is greatly faster.

Copy mode briefly extends the boot time to gain some of the RAM-run speed of default mode and the persistence of a pure mount mode.

In copy mode, it is important to note that extensions can be either mounted or copied into RAM. The Apps program makes this flexibility possible by keeping track of user selections.

It should be noted that using a bulk selection, that is, loading all extensions to RAM, allows the storage to be unmounted, and the system to avoid any corruption on power loss.

1.10. Backup/restore & other persistence options

Aside from the mount mode and the **tce** directory of application extensions, Tiny Core supports persistent/permanent:

• backup and restore of personal settings, and

• persistent /home and /opt directories.

1.10.1. Backup/restore

Tiny Core includes the filetool utility for saving personal settings and data. The text file **/opt/.filetool.lst** lists files and directories to be backed up at power down and restored at reboot. The list may be changed manually (using vi, nano, etc) or via the scripts in the Tools menu; note that the entry for **/opt/.filetool.lst** should never be removed from the list itself. Filetool also supports exclusion of particular files via **/opt/.xfiletool.lst**.

By default, **filetool.lst** includes the entire home/tc directory, and **xfiletool.lst** excludes some unnecessary caches and temporary directories.

Filetool writes the backup file **mydata.tgz**. The location of mydata.tgz can be initially set using the boot option **restore=hdXY**, **restore=hdXY/directory**, or, after boot, by selecting Backup/ Restore from the Control Panel. If the restore code is not used, Tiny Core will search for **mydata.tgz** in available root directories at boot. Conversely, the boot option **norestore** ignores any existing backup files, a useful tool for troubleshooting and upgrading.

Further settings and configurations are stored or executed using /home/tc/.xsession, /home/tc/.profile, /opt/bootlocal.sh, and /opt.

1.10.2. Persistent home

Just as Tiny Core offers persistence options for downloaded application extensions, so does it for your home directory. These are set using boot codes/options.

The bootcode **home=hdXY** will automatically setup /home/tc to "bind" to /mnt/hdXY/home/tc. The home boot code lets Tiny Core coexist with other Linux installations by inserting the tc user directory under a pre-existing /home directory. Also, Tiny Core cannot auto-detect a persistent home directory, so the home boot option is always required.

The decision on whether to use the default backup, or to set up a persistent home/opt directory depends on the amount of data you intend to save, and the device you use for storage (USB flash and SSDs may have limited write cycles, for instance).

1.11. Bottom line

If you have made it this far, congratulations! You're ready to get Tiny Core and get started. Browse the wiki, the forums, the download pages, and join the community conversation.

Welcome from the Tiny Core Team.

Chapter 2. Installing

A Core install consists of three parts: a bootloader on some media, the main image (kernel and **core.gz**) on some media, and the **tce** directory on some media.

While these can all be on the same disk, they need not be; all three can be on separate media if needed.

 A Core install is completely nomadic, it doesn't read any settings from the install system.

This means you can install to a drive on one system, and then move the drive to the target system without any issues. This is useful for example for laptops that can't boot from CD or USB.

2.1. With the official installer

The official installer is included in the Core Plus edition, but can also be downloaded separately to install from a TinyCore or a command-line Core image (**tc-install.tcz**).

The command-line version, **tc-install.sh**, is not covered here, but it follows the same prompts as the graphical version.

The GUI installer is a five-step process.

2.1.1. Step 1: Source and destination

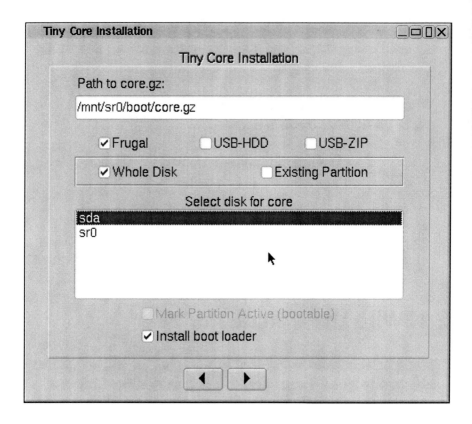

In the first step, we need to select the install media, install type, and the target. The installer may be able to detect the install media automatically as in this image; if not, click on the "Path to core.gz" text field to browse for the install media.

The three install types are frugal, USB-HDD, and USB-ZIP. Frugal is the default type, it may be installed to a partition, and usually works for bootable USB sticks too. USB-HDD uses the whole disk and slightly different formatting, which may help the USB stick boot on computers it otherwise wouldn't. USB-ZIP is for older BIOSes that needed ZIP-drive emulation in order to boot from USB.

If this is the only Linux system on the computer, select "Install boot loader" and "Mark partition active" (the latter only if not using the whole disk).

2.1.2. Step 2: File system type

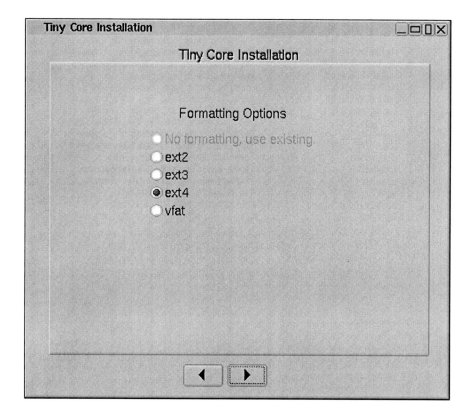

Here we select the formatting, defaulting to ext4.

2.1.3. Step 3: Boot codes

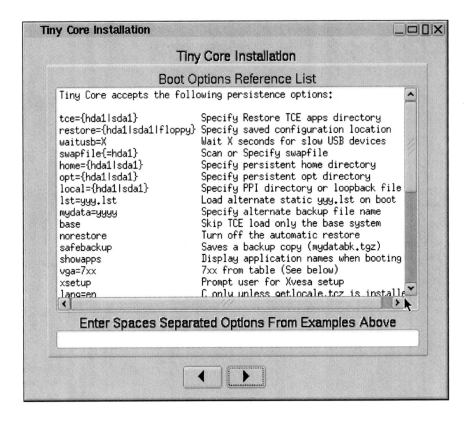

```
Tiny Core Installation                                    _ □ □ X

                      Tiny Core Installation

                   Boot Options Reference List
  Tiny Core accepts the following persistence options:      ▲

  tce={hda1|sda1}             Specify Restore TCE apps directory
  restore={hda1|sda1|floppy}  Specify saved configuration location
  waitusb=X                   Wait X seconds for slow USB devices
  swapfile{=hda1}             Scan or Specify swapfile
  home={hda1|sda1}            Specify persistent home directory
  opt={hda1|sda1}             Specify persistent opt directory
  local={hda1|sda1}           Specify PPI directory or loopback file
  lst=yyy.lst                 Load alternate static yyy.lst on boot
  mydata=yyyy                 Specify alternate backup file name
  base                        Skip TCE load only the base system
  norestore                   Turn off the automatic restore
  safebackup                  Saves a backup copy (mydatabk.tgz)
  showapps                    Display application names when booting
  vga=7xx                     7xx from table (See below)
  xsetup                      Prompt user for Xvesa setup
  lang=en                     C only unless getlocale.tcz is installe ▼
  ◄                                                           ► ►

      Enter Spaces Separated Options From Examples Above


  ┌──────────────────────────────────────────────────────────┐
  └──────────────────────────────────────────────────────────┘


                       ◄      ►
```

If you want to enter any boot codes, this is the place. By default you don't need any.

You can change these later by editing the bootloader config file.

2.1.4. Step 4: Optional parts

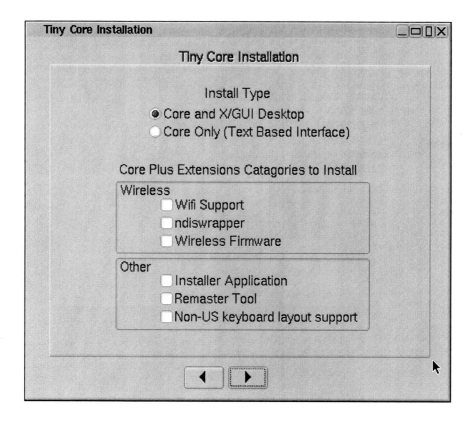

This page is only visible when installing from the Core Plus image. You can choose to install some useful extensions here. They can be installed afterwards too, this choice is not special or irreversible.

2.1.5. Step 5: Good to go?

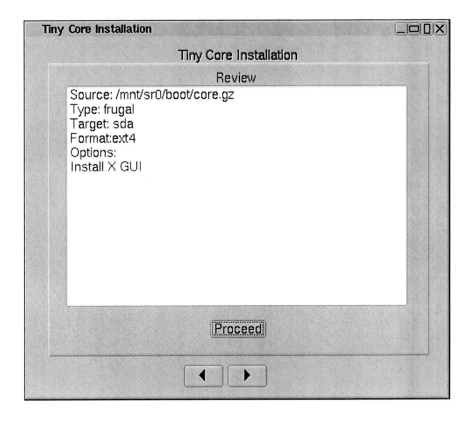

In the final step, the installer lets us review the choices before starting. If everything's in order, click Proceed.

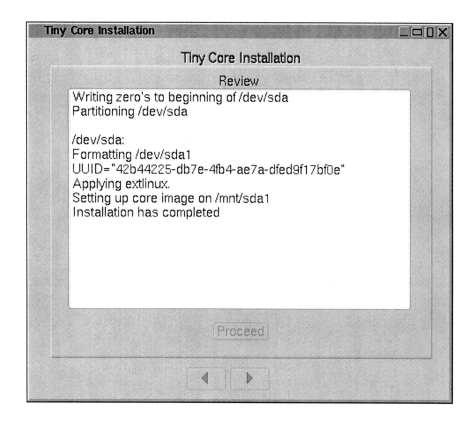

The installer will happily chug away, and assuming nothing out of place happens, you'll see a success screen like the one above. Ready to reboot to Core?

```
Booting Core 4.7.7
Running Linux Kernel 3.0.21-tinycore.
Checking boot options...Done.
Starting udev daemon for hotplug support...Done.
Scanning hard disk partitions to create /etc/fstab
Setting Language to C Done.
Possible swap partition(s) enabled.
Loading extensions...Done.
Setting keymap to us Done.
Setting hostname to box Done.
_
```

2.2. From Windows via core2usb

Core Team member bmarkus created a simple USB installer for Windows users. It's not recommended to use third-party installers such as LiLi or Unetbootin, as they won't create the third part of the install (the **tce** directory), meaning more work for you.

This utility is available from http://core2usb.sf.net/. If you don't want to burn a CD, it's a convenient one-click way to install Core to USB.

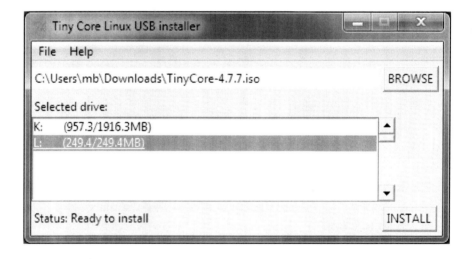

2.3. Manually

A manual install can be done from any Linux distro. For advanced users it's often faster than burning a CD or otherwise installing via the installer.

As the exact steps vary a lot depending on your program and host distro choices, we'll only cover the general parts here.

2.3.1. Step 1: Partitioning & formatting

BIOS installations

Create a normal partition on the target disk using your favorite program: for GUI we recommend **Gparted**, for command line **cfdisk**; both should be available in all major distros.

The partition should be formatted with a Linux file system. We recommend **ext4** for general use. If the target is an USB stick or other media with limited writes, you may want to use **ext2** instead, as journaling file systems do extra writes to preserve integrity.

If the target is a regular hard disk, it's recommended to also create and format a swap partition.

Using more exotic file systems like XFS needs either a remaster or some other way to load the XFS support, in order to access the XFS partition.

UEFI installations

Create a GPT EFI boot partition and a normal partition using your favorite program: for GUI we recommend **Gparted**, for command line **gdisk**; both should be available in all major distros.

The EFI partition should be formatted with vfat and the normal partition should be formatted with a Linux file system.

Older Apple machines typically use 32-bit EFI whereas more modern Apple machines and PC hardware use 64-bit (U)EFI. This means that you will need to use either core64 or corepure64 with 64-bit (U)EFI installations.

2.3.2. Step 2: Files

The latest Core files are available separately for your convenience - no need to unpack them from the ISO file. Download **core.gz** and **vmlinuz** from your closest mirror, from the directory **release/distribution_files**. The link for the main mirror is http://repo.tinycorelinux.net/4.x/x86/release/distribution_files/.

The usual location for the kernel and initrd is under /boot on the target partition, but you can place them anywhere.

To hold your extensions, create a root directory called **tce** on the target partition.

2.3.3. Step 3: Bootloader

Finally, you need to install a bootloader to the target disk's MBR, and point it to the kernel and initrd.

For BIOS installs, the syslinux family, lilo, grub 0.x, and grub 2 have been tested to work fine. For UEFI installs, only grub 2 has been tested.

For a normal boot, no boot codes need to be added - the location of the **tce** directory will be autodetected. If you anticipate having multiple **tce** directories, then it's recommended to specify which one you want as a boot code.

For USB sticks, and other removable/slow media such as SD cards, you might need to add the **waitusb** bootcode. It tells Core to wait the given number of seconds to give slow devices time to register, and optionally polls for a given partition label or UUID to proceed as soon as the device shows up.

The syntax is **waitusb=5** to wait five seconds, or **waitusb=20:LABEL=mydisk** to wait up to twenty seconds for the partition labeled "mydisk" to show up.

Finally, you might want to limit the kernel's boot output by adding the **quiet** bootcode.

A typical grub 0.97 config file might look like this:

```
default 0
timeout 10

title Core
root (hd0,0)
kernel /boot/vmlinuz quiet waitusb=5
initrd /boot/core.gz
```

Likewise, a typical grub 2 config file (with the partition's UUID replaced):

```
search --no-floppy --fs-uuid --set=root "fdsf-gt434"

menuentry "Core" {
  linux /boot/vmlinuz quiet waitusb=5
  initrd /boot/core.gz
}
```

Chapter 3. Basic package management via GUI

The first contact is often the graphical package manager, the Apps tool. You can start it from the bottom launcher under the name Apps, or if using an alternate window manager without wbar, under the menu.

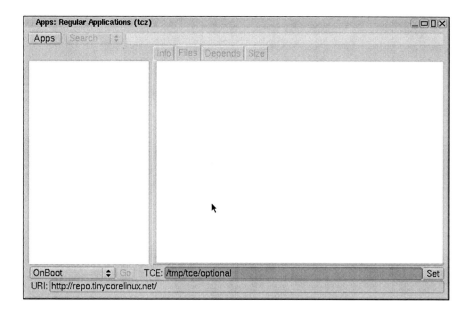

Let's quickly go over the interface.

The two white main areas are for the content. On the left, once connected, you will have a list of packages, while the right panel displays the info you've selected from the four tabs.

The tabs are respectively the extension's info file, the list of files in the extension, the list of dependencies, and an analysis of the total download size needed.

The drop-down menu on the bottom, currently saying "OnBoot", defines what to do with the selected extension. The modes will be covered later on in detail.

The tce bar displays the path to your current **tce** directory. If it's the default (RAM), it will be red; if it's on permanent storage, it will be green. The set button to the right lets you set the **tce** directory if needed.

The URI bar shows the selected mirror.

The search drop-down menu lets you do three kinds of searches: by name, by tag, and by the files it provides.

Finally, the main menu in the upper-left corner defines the mode of action.

To start browsing, click on the Apps menu - remote - browse.

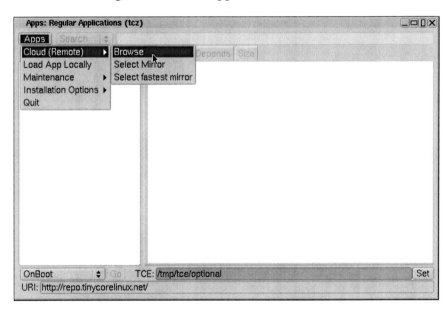

We can browse the full list, or get a list of search results with the upper-right search bar. To return to the full list from a search results list, click again on remote - browse.

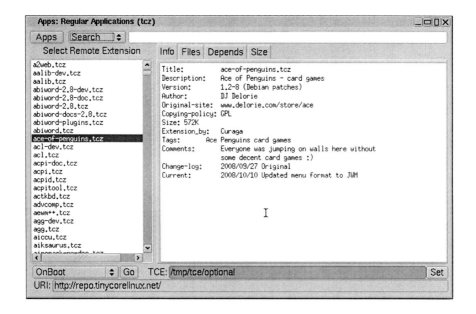

With Ace of Penguins selected, we are shown the info file by default. If we're interested in the files, dependencies, or how much we'd need to download, the tabs are now active.

Let's go on to install it. But with which method?

Install methods

OnBoot
> The default method. This extension will be installed, and added to the onboot list, to be mounted on the following boots.

OnDemand
> A loading script will be generated for this extension. Instead of being loaded on boot, the icon/menu entry for this extension will load the extension when you first need it.
> This option speeds up your boot time, at the cost of making the first start of the application slower.

Download + load

> The extension will be downloaded and installed for this session only. If you have set up your **tce** directory, it will reside there, but since it is not added to the onboot list, it will not be loaded after a reboot.

Download only

> The extension will only be downloaded, nothing more will be done.

Let's pick OnBoot today, the default. Clicking on Go, a download progress window will pop up, and soon we're informed that the install succeeded:

Should the install fail (network error, md5sum failure...), you will be informed of the issue with a popup.

Let's enjoy a well deserved game of penguin FreeCell now:

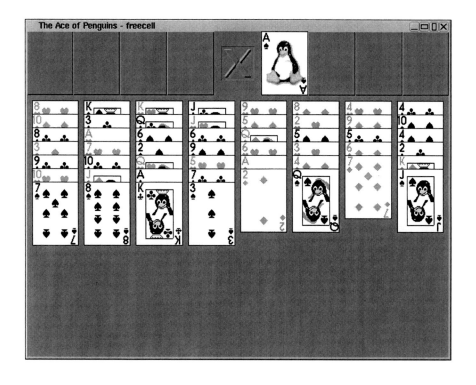

Chapter 4. Basic package management via CLI

In this chapter we'll go over the basic use of the command line equivalent to Apps, **tce-ab**, and the direct interface, **tce-load**.

Starting tce-ab, we are greeted with a line-based interface:

```
$ tce-ab
tce-ab - Tiny Core Extension: Application Browser

S)earch P)rovides K)eywords Q)uit:
```

The three search options are the same as with the Apps program (note that keywords = tags).

For example, doing a keyword search for "browser", we are greeted with a list of extensions with a matching tag. Selecting the number of the extension fires up the extension's info file in the **less** viewer.

```
tce - Tiny Core Extension browser

         1. appbrowser-cli.tcz
         2. arora.tcz
         3. bonecho-gtk2.tcz
         4. bonecho.tcz
         5. chimera2.tcz
         6. chromium-browser-locale.tcz
         7. chromium-browser.tcz
         8. conkeror.tcz
         9. dillo2-doc.tcz
        10. dillo3-doc.tcz
        11. dillo3-ssl-doc.tcz
        12. dillo3-ssl.tcz
        13. dillo3.tcz
        14. dooble.tcz
        15. dwb.tcz

Enter selection ( 1 - 80 ) or (q)uit, (n)ext, \
(p)revious:
```

After having read the info file and pressing *q* to quit **less**, tce-ab gives us a set of choices on what to do with it:

```
A)bout I)nstall O)nDemand D)epends T)ree F)iles siZ)e \
L)ist S)earch P)rovides K)eywords Q)uit:
```

About brings us back to the info file, install and ondemand have the same functions as with Apps, as do depends, files and size. Displaying the tree file will show the recursive chart of dependencies, used by the size function to calculate the necessary download size.

List will return us to the selection list, and the search options will let us to do a new search.

4.1. tce-load

Tce-load is the non-interactive tool used behind the scenes by the boot process, Apps, and tce-ab.

Running it with the help option gives us a short overview of what it does:

```
$ tce-load -h
Usage: tce-load [-i -w -wi -wo -wil -ic -wic]{s} \
extensions
   -i    Loads local extension
   -w    Download extension only
   -wi   Download and install extension
   -wo   Download and create an ondemand item
   Adding -c to any -i option will force a one time \
       copy to file system
   Adding -l to any -i option indicates load only - \
       do not update onboot or ondemand
   Adding -s to any option will suppress OK message \
       used by apps GUI

Example usage:
 Load local extension:
   tce-load -i /mnt/hda1/tce/optional/nano.tcz
 Download into tce/optional directory, updates OnBoot
and installs:
   tce-load -w -i nano.tcz
 Download only into tce/optional directory:
   tce-load -w nano.tcz
```

For example, if we already know the name of the extension needed, we can ask for it to be downloaded and installed (the OnBoot mode):

```
$ tce-load -wi ace-of-penguins
```

The tool will operate in the set **tce** directory, so unless given full path, it will look there first. Suppose we had selected "Download only" for Ace of Penguins before, and thus it was not installed for this session. We could install it with:

```
$ tce-load -i ace-of-penguins
```

 Just like most Core tools, tce-load and tce-ab are shell scripts. As far as package managers go, they are fairly simple and easy to understand.

You are encouraged to look under the hood.

4.2. Comparing package managers

	apt (deb)	yum (rpm)	tce-load (tcz)
Install a package from the repo	apt-get install **pkg**	yum install **pkg**	tce-load -wi **pkg**
Install from a local file	dpkg -i **pkg**	yum localinstall **pkg**	tce-load -i **pkg**
Search	apt-cache search **pattern**	yum search **pattern**	tce-ab
List installed packages	dpkg -l	rpm -qa	ls /usr/local/ tce.installed

Chapter 5. Updating the base system

As new minor and patch versions are released, for example 4.7 and 4.7.1, how do we update to the latest core?

The process is usually as simple as downloading the latest vmlinuz and core.gz, and replacing them on your boot media. This can be done live from the system, as Tiny Core boots to RAM, and so you can operate on the boot files in any way you wish.

After a reboot, you will be running the latest core code. To check the running version, you can run the **version** command:

```
$ version
4.7.5
```

It is important to review the release notes for any items in your backup that may need to be updated. Often there are tweaks to the user files such as .profile, which you may have customized to your needs; any such files are mentioned in the release notes.

The latest pristine copies of any user files can be found in **/etc/skel**. If you have customized some of the files, please compare the latest copy with your version to see if any changes need to be done.

With the base system updated, it's recommended to update extensions next.

Chapter 6. Updating extensions

Extensions are usually updated more often than the base system.

As extension updates may require some action on your part, it is recommended to view the info files of updated extensions before doing the update. The Apps tool will let you do that, while the command-line update is a batch one.

In both cases, the updated extensions are stored in a staging directory, and the actual update will be applied on the next reboot. This ensures that no running app will be interfered with by things being changed from under it.

6.1. Apps

Starting with the GUI update method, fire up Apps, and select Apps - Maintenance - Check for updates.

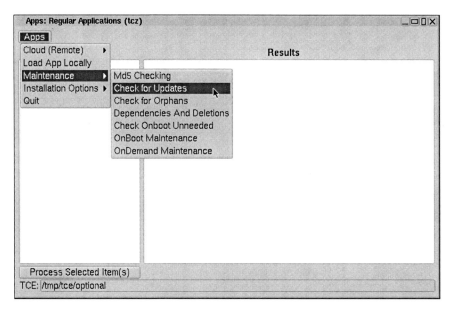

After a short while, Apps will have the left panel populated with all extensions with available updates, with the status from the check displayed in the right panel.

If there is a newer Core version available, or some of the extensions have been removed from the repository, this information will be shown in the right panel.

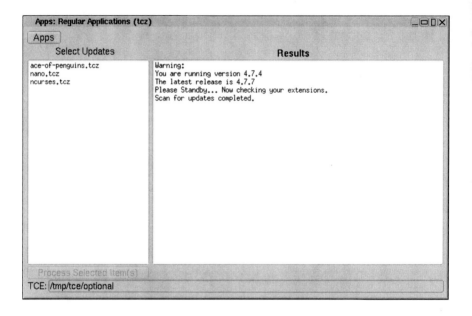

Clicking on an item will show that extension's info file: whether the update is just a bog-standard version update, or whether some action is required will be visible there.

To select all items for processing, pick the first one, hold shift, and pick the last one. Clicking on "Process selected item(s)" will start the update.

6.2. tce-update

Simply running **sudo tce-update** will do a batch update of all extensions.

However, if there is not enough space to store the updated extensions, you will need to do an in-place update, which requires a boot with the boot codes **base norestore**. These options cause no extensions to be loaded, making it safe to write the files directly.

The script will warn you and exit, if the space is too tight to do a normal update.

Chapter 7. Persistence

With the many options for making your data persistent and not disappearing on power-off, it might be a bit confusing to decide which to use. In this chapter we will go over all the options, listing their pros and cons, and the most common setup.

7.1. Backup

The backup is on by default as long as you have set up a **tce** directory. It will save all your personal files in your home directory, and the system config files under /opt, excluding common browser caches.

So all is well, right? The data is safe, restored on boot, saved on power-off. However, as backup happens in those two spots, having a large amount of data will slow down your boot and shutdown process.

The backup is ideal for when you have a small amount of data to save, such as application config files or browser bookmarks. A few ten megabytes of PDFs on the other hand will be slow.

The other angle is the number of writes. With backup, the storage media is only written to on shutdown. This is excellent if the media happens to be a device with limited writes, such as USB flash, SSD, Compact Flash/Secure Digital memory card, or similar.

No action is needed to use backup as long as a **tce** directory is setup; you will be asked in the shutdown dialog whether to do backup, and the box is ticked by default.

 If not doing backup is more common for you, you can change the default to be unticked by adding the line BACKUP=0 to your .profile.

The backup is controlled by two files in /opt: **.filetool.lst** lists everything to include, and **.xfiletool.lst** lists everything to exclude. Exclusions will override inclusions.

For the syntax of these files, see the documentation on tar.

7.2. Persistent home/opt

If you have more data to store in these locations, for example personal documents in /home or a third-party binary application in /opt, it's recommended to use persistence for these locations.

The file system on the partition needs to support linux permissions; FAT and NTFS will not work.

However, every write to these locations will then go directly to the device, so unless the device is a hard drive, you'll need to weigh on how often it is written. For the "big binary installed in /opt" case, writes would be rare; but for the home directory, all kinds of apps will have caches, configuration files, and other data there they will update.

To make use of these options, you need to add a bootcode for each. You may specify the device directly, via UUID, or via its label.

For example, to use the sda1 partition for home, and sda2 for opt, the boot codes would be **home=sda1 opt=sda2**.

Using absolute names can be unreliable if there are multiple drives present; how fast they initialize affects their naming. So if there are multiple internal drives, or you wish to use an external drive, it's recommended to use either UUID or label.

With a partition labeled "HomeDrive", the home bootcode would be **home=LABEL=HomeDrive**. With a partition's UUID, the bootcode would be **home=UUID=f4t4-65467yg-6546**.

You can view the attached drives' labels and UUIDs with the **blkid** command.

 When using either of these options, you need to remove the corresponding directory from /opt/.filetool.lst. Otherwise it is both backed up and stored directly, removing any benefits of either.

7.3. Personal extension

If you have read-only data that needs to be in the file system, it's recommended to make a personal extension out of it instead of keeping it in the backup.

For more details on this option, see the Creating extensions chapter.

7.4. Other data storage

In no way are you restricted to just these options; storing your data is completely up to how you want to do it.

For example, say you have a few gigabytes of music stored in sda1/ music. You could add a symlink there to your home directory, file manager, or many other ways; here, we'll symlink it as /music, so that it's nicely accessible to any application.

If the drive is an internal one, with a stable name, you can just add the symlink to your backup. The backup process will only save the symlink, it will not descend into the pointed directory.

If the music drive's name might change, it is better to create the symlink in bootlocal.sh based on the drive's label for example. For more information on bootlocal.sh, see the Boot process chapter.

7.5. Common setup

With the alternatives listed, what is the common setup?

The common setup is one hard drive, persistent home, backup, and optionally other links there.

To set this up on an installed system, you only need to add the **home=sda1** bootcode to your bootloader's config file (where sda1 is your partition), and reboot. To see that it's being used, type **mount**.

7.6. Summary

Backup

- Happens on boot and shutdown

- Slow if you have lots of data

Persistent home/opt

- Direct writes

- No boot overhead

Personal extension

- Only static data

- Very little boot overhead

Any combinations are allowed.

Chapter 8. Managing extensions

This chapter will detail the options under the Maintenance menu in Apps.

8.1. MD5 checking

This option allows you to do a corruption check for downloaded extensions. Many types of corruption are detected when trying to install an extension, but for some types, it can be useful to do a manual check.

8.2. Check for orphans

Orphans are extensions not found in the repository. They may have been removed for various reasons, or they may be custom extensions not submitted to the repository.

You aren't required to take any action in case an extension was removed from the mirrors; if it works for you, you can continue to use it, but no updates will be coming.

8.3. Dependencies and deletions

This mode lets you view various reports on the dependencies of all extensions present in the tce directory. Some may require the reporting database to be build, those will be greyed out until the helper database is built.

One function in particular, update dep files, is occasionally needed. Occasionally there's server-side reorganization of the dependencies, or an extension may be renamed, requiring you to update the dependency files to avoid inconsistencies. After updating the .dep files, it's recommended to use the "Fetch missing dependencies", in case a dependency was added, or an extension was renamed.

The other function, extension deletion, allows you to mark an extension to be deleted on the next reboot. All of their dependencies that aren't needed by anything else will also be removed.

8.4. Check onboot unneeded

This option analyzes your onboot.lst to see if there are any redundant items. For example, gtk2 is a dependency of Firefox, so if you listed both gtk2 and Firefox, gtk2 would be redundant.

Having a compact list without such redundancies helps boot time.

8.5. Onboot/ondemand maintenance

These two modes allow you to add and remove extensions from the onboot or ondemand lists. This comes in handy if you earlier chose to have an extension be on demand, but now it would make more sense to load it on boot, for example.

Onboot.lst is a plain text file, so you can edit it with an editor of your choice in addition to the GUI method listed. Ondemand items are generated scripts, so managing them manually is discouraged.

Chapter 9. Virtualization - Core as a guest

Most virtual machines default to emulating actual, common hardware. Core should run directly on any of those. However, some default to server hardware, and many have special virtualization-only hardware that can improve performance. This chapter explores these gotchas.

9.1. Qemu / KVM

The premier open source virtualization solution, KVM, runs Core splendidly. There's built-in support for most of the virtio drivers, helping the virtual machine reach faster performance.

To make use of the virtio network card, add **-net nic,model=virtio -net user** to your Qemu command line. If you have a special network setup (other than user), don't add the **-net user** part.

To use a virtio disk, instead of the common **-hda file**, the syntax is **-drive file=file,if=virtio,media=disk**. Use **media=cdrom** for ISO images instead.

The default options to adjust the assigned RAM and CPU cores work fine; **-m 256 -smp 4** would give the VM 256 megabytes of RAM and four cores.

The absolute pointer mode, enabled via **-usb -usbdevice tablet**, does not work perfectly with Xvesa, but works fine when using Xorg.

9.2. Virtualbox

Virtualbox shares some code with Qemu, and it can also use the virtio network and block drivers; enable them from the settings.

The mouse support in early Virtualbox 4 releases was broken with Xvesa as far as we know; using Xorg or Virtualbox 3 instead are workarounds.

In current Virtualbox 4 releases, disabling the **absolute pointing device** and using the key-based switching allows the mouse to work properly.

9.3. VMWare

VMWare's virtualized network card and SCSI card are supported (vmxnet3 and pvscsi). However, VMWare defaults to an emulated SCSI card whose support is not built-in, but included in the **scsi** extension - a catch 22 situation. In order to load extensions from a SCSI drive, one would need to create a remaster that includes the SCSI drivers, or to have a two-step boot with the SCSI drivers on an IDE disk.

The best way is to choose the paravirtualized option for network and SCSI card though, as they will work directly.

9.4. HyperV

Microsoft HyperV Linux support was still quite unstable during the time of Core 4.x; it is not supported. HyperV is supported in the coming 5.x versions.

Chapter 10. Bootcodes explained

Boot codes are a way to configure the system, by giving it information that needs to be available during boot. In this chapter we will cover each in detail.

The Linux kernel also exposes a set of boot codes; these will not be covered here.

When using the CD, you can enter them at the command line (with the Core ISO) or by pressing **tab** (with the TinyCore or CorePlus ISOs) at the desired menu item. On an installed system, they are stored in your bootloader's configuration file.

For example, with **grub 0.97**, the file is called **menu.lst**, and the boot codes are stored on the kernel line:

```
kernel /boot/vmlinuz quiet showapps
```

If using extlinux, the file is called **extlinux.cfg**, and the codes are stored in the APPEND line:

```
APPEND initrd=/boot/core.gz quiet showapps
```

10.1. tce - extensions directory

The **tce** bootcode specifies where to locate and store the extensions and backup. If it's not given, the system will scan all drives for a first-level directory called **/tce**. Thus it may improve boot time to specify where it is.

It needs to be given when there are multiple such directories (for example to use your USB installation even on machines with Core on the hard disk), or if the directory is not named **tce**.

The bootcode supports both labels and UUIDs (universal identifiers), which are a necessity with USB drives, as you can't tell beforehand how the USB stick might get named.

Examples:

- tce=sda1

- tce=sda1/mydir

- tce=LABEL=mydisk

- tce=LABEL=mydisk/mydir

- tce=UUID=fho4-3436t

- tce=UUID=fho4-3436t/mydir

10.2. restore - backup location

If you wish to store the backup in a separate location (ie. not under the **tce** directory), you need to use the **restore** bootcode.

Example:

- restore=sda1

10.3. waitusb - slow drive detection

Many USB drives are very slow to be detected. Even if plugged in before boot, they may take ten seconds to initialize - longer than the system would take to boot.

The **waitusb** bootcode allows you to tell the system to wait, either for a specific drive, or a given number of seconds.

When waiting for a specific drive, both labels and UUIDs are accepted.

Examples:

- waitusb=5

- waitusb=15:LABEL=mydisk

- waitusb=15:UUID=fho4-3436t

The first form waits five seconds in all cases. The second form waits up to 15 seconds, continuing immediately if the drive with the label "mydisk" shows up.

10.4. swapfile - swap in a file

In normal use, you would use a regular Linux swap partition. However, if the system is installed to a fat32 partition, and you cannot create a swap partition, you may use a swap file. It is created with the GUI tool, and the bootcode is used to tell the system to use it.

Examples:

- swapfile

- swapfile=sda1

The first form will scan for a swap file, the second will scan for it only in the specified drive.

10.5. home and opt - persistence

The **home** and **opt** bootcodes let you keep the respective directories on a persistent disk. Each bootcode takes either a drive name, a label, or an UUID.

These options are covered in more detail in the persistence chapter.

Examples:

- home=sda1

- home=LABEL=mydisk

- home=UUID=fho4-3436t

10.6. lst - extension list

By default, the system loads all extensions in the list **onboot.lst**. Using the **lst** bootcode, you can tell the system to use another list. The list is expected to be in the **tce** directory, just like **onboot.lst**.

This is used for example to load different setups via a boot menu: a quick music environment wouldn't need web browsers.

Example:

- lst=myfile.lst

10.7. base - don't load extensions

In case you don't want to load extensions, the **base** bootcode skips them. It may be used as a restore option, as when combined with the **norestore** option, no drives are mounted during the boot process.

Example:

- base

10.8. norestore - don't load backup

To get a pristine environment without your settings, you can use the **norestore** bootcode. It's useful to see if something also happens in a new configuration, for example. When combined with the **base** bootcode, no drives are mounted during boot.

Example:

- norestore

10.9. safebackup - enable safe backup by default

While you can select the safe backup from the backup GUI, this boot option forces it to always be used. The safe backup means that a copy of your previous backup is made before doing a new backup.

Example:

- safebackup

10.10. showapps - verbose extension loading

By default, the loaded extensions are not listed. This bootcode has the system show each extension by name when loading it. It slightly delays the boot, but it's useful to find which extension has trouble loading, if one has become corrupted, for example.

Example:

- showapps

10.11. iso - load extensions from an ISO file

This boot option tells the system to load extensions from an ISO file. It's useful for some virtual setups, and the syslinux memdisk option (as only DOS-based systems can read the memory disk after boot).

Examples:

- iso=sda1

- iso=sda1/dir/TinyCore-4.4.iso

10.12. vga - framebuffer resolution

	640x480	800x600	1024x768	1280x1024
256 colors	769	771	773	775
16-bit	785	788	791	794
24-bit	786	789	792	795

By default, the system boots in VGA text mode (80x25). To get a higher-resolution console, you can give one of the options above. The framebuffer can also be used as a graphical fallback system with the Xfbdev server, in case the normal VESA server fails to work.

Example:

- vga=791

10.13. xsetup - configure X during boot

While the X setup script, **xsetup**, may be launched after boot too, this bootcode tells the system to launch it during boot. The wizard lets you choose the resolution and mouse settings.

Example:

- xsetup

10.14. lang - system locale

If you have generated your preferred locale using the **getlocale.tcz** extension, you can use this bootcode to enable it. With a custom locale, numbers, dates and so on will be printed in your local convention, and all applications that are translated to your language will use that language.

If not set, the default C locale is used (US English, ASCII).

Example:

- lang=fi_FI

10.15. kmap - console keymap

If you have **kmaps.tcz** installed, you can use this bootcode to set the default console keymap. The console keymap is also used by the tiny X servers (Xvesa and Xfbdev), but not the larger X server Xorg.

If not set, the default is used (US).

Example:

- kmap=qwerty/fi-latin9

10.16. text - boot to text mode

In case an X server is installed, do not boot to graphical mode. If an X server is not installed, the system will always boot to text mode.

Example:

- text

10.17. superuser - boot to text mode, as root

Like the **text** bootcode above, but boots to a root shell.

Example:

- superuser

10.18. noicons - don't display icons

This bootcode will disable the default icon bar, or optionally only ondemand icons.

Examples:

- noicons

- noicons=ondemand

10.19. noswap - don't use the swap partition

By default, the system will use all Linux swap partitions automatically. This bootcode will disable their use.

Example:

- noswap

10.20. nodhcp - don't grab an IP address

The system will use DHCP to get an IP address by default. If you wish to set the IP manually, you can use this bootcode to skip the DHCP process.

Example:

- nodhcp

10.21. noutc - BIOS is using local time

In case your BIOS is set to your local time and not UTC (GMT)
time, use this boot code.

Example:

- noutc

10.22. tz - timezone

This bootcode lets you manually specify your time zone.

Example:

- tz=GMT-8

10.23. pause - wait for a keypress before completing boot

This bootcode lets you view the system boot messages more easily,
by waiting for an enter key press before completing the boot.

Example:

- pause

10.24. cron and syslog - start daemons

The **cron** and **syslog** bootcodes will start the respective daemon at
boot. By default neither is running.

Example:

- cron

- syslog

10.25. host - set host name

By default the host name is "box". This bootcode lets you set a custom one.

Example:

- host=foo

10.26. protect - use encrypted backup

The default backup is a normal archive file. This option lets you encrypt the backup using Blowfish with a 448-bit key, generated from the given passphrase. If not using a persistent home, all your custom configuration will be in the backup, so this option prevents someone from reading your backup off the drive.

Example:

- protect

10.27. secure - set password on boot

If you need to set the password on boot, for example on a first run, use this bootcode.

Example:

- secure

10.28. noautologin - disable automatic login

With this boot code, the system will not log in, but instead ask for username and password.

Example:

- noautologin

10.29. user - set the default username

The default user is normally named *tc*. This bootcode lets you use a different name.

Example:

- user=john

10.30. desktop - specify window manager

If only one window manager is installed, that one will be used. If you have multiple window managers installed, this bootcode will let you specify which one to load.

Example:

- desktop=fluxbox

10.31. laptop - force loading of laptop modules

Usually these modules are autodetected, but if your laptop does not load the modules (AC, battery, and PCMCIA), you can add this bootcode to force-load them.

Example:

- laptop

10.32. noembed - use a separate tmpfs

This is an advanced option that changes where in RAM Core is run from. By default, Core uses the tmpfs setup by the kernel; with this bootcode, Core will setup a new tmpfs file system, and use that instead.

Using this bootcode temporarily doubles the RAM use, as both copies are kept in RAM at once during boot. As an extra copy is made, it also slows the boot time. It allows GNU df to detect the free space in /, used by some proprietary software installers.

Example:

- noembed

10.33. nozswap - disable compressed swap in RAM

By default, Core uses a RAM compression technique allowing you to use more RAM than you actually have. If you experience problems with this, the **nozswap** bootcode lets you disable this.

Example:

- nozswap

10.34. xvesa - set resolution directly

This bootcode lets you specify the resolution for Xvesa directly.

Example:

- xvesa=800x600x32

10.35. mydata - use a different name for backup

By default, the backup is named mydata.tgz. Using this boot code you can use a different name.

Example:

- mydata=command.com

10.36. blacklist - blacklist modules

Occasionally a module for your hardware is loaded, but you don't want it to load. In these cases, you can blacklist it.

One prominent example is the PC speaker. Some people love the beeps, others hate them. To blacklist multiple modules, you can use either multiple **blacklist** bootcodes, or give a comma-separated list.

Examples:

- blacklist=pcspkr

- blacklist=pcspkr,e100

10.37. multivt - setup multiple consoles

By default, the system saves RAM by only setting up one console. Using this option, the more common amount of six consoles gets setup.

Example:

- multivt

Part II. Advanced use

Chapter 11. Remastering

Remastering is the process of editing the initrd image. Producing a new ISO image is not necessary, but is often useful if you intend to burn the result to a CD or to test easily in a virtual machine.

This chapter covers the process of remastering manually. There exists a helper extension, EZRemaster, but that one will not be covered here.

You typically only need to remaster if you need to edit any of the early boot scripts, or if intending to create a stand-alone image for a specific deployment that runs entirely in RAM. As updating a remastered image to a newer Core version can be a hassle, a method for that is covered in the next chapter.

11.1. Prerequisites

You need a Linux distribution with the required programs available: cpio, tar, gzip, advdef, and mkisofs. This need not be Tiny Core itself, but remastering inside Tiny Core is the most tested option.

For remastering on Core, install the extensions **advcomp.tcz** and optionally **mkisofs-tools.tcz** if creating an ISO image.

11.2. Unpacking

First, we'll extract the kernel and initrd image from the latest Core ISO.

```
$ sudo mkdir /mnt/tmp
$ sudo mount TinyCore-current.iso /mnt/tmp -o loop,ro
$ cd /mnt/tmp
$ cp boot/vmlinuz boot/tinycore.gz /tmp
$ sudo umount /mnt/tmp
```

If you are going to create an ISO image, instead of copying only these two files, copy everything:

```
$ sudo mkdir /mnt/tmp
$ sudo mount TinyCore-current.iso /mnt/tmp -o loop,ro
$ cp -a /mnt/tmp/boot /tmp
$ mv /tmp/boot/tinycore.gz /tmp
$ sudo umount /mnt/tmp
```

With the files copied into /tmp, we'll be unpacking the initrd image next.

```
$ sudo mkdir /tmp/extract
$ cd /tmp/extract
$ zcat /tmp/tinycore.gz | sudo cpio -i -H newc -d
```

Please note the use of sudo where needed; root rights are required to preserve permissions correctly. If your host distribution sets non-default flags for **/tmp**, you may also need to change the permissions of the **/tmp/extract** directory - it needs to be **root:root 755** in order to produce a bootable image.

Now, with the initrd image laid bare before our eyes, feel free to do any edits, additions, or removals needed.

11.3. Packing

With the modifications done, these steps create the initrd image from the extracted directory tree:

```
$ cd /tmp/extract
$ sudo find | sudo cpio -o -H newc | \
  gzip -2 > ../tinycore.gz
$ cd /tmp
$ advdef -z4 tinycore.gz
```

The image is compressed using gzip's level 2 to save time. Advdef is used to re-compress the image with a slightly better implementation, producing a smaller image that is faster to boot.

11.4. Creating an ISO image

The following commands create a bootable ISO image, ready to be burned or booted in a virtual machine:

```
$ cd /tmp
$ mv tinycore.gz boot
$ mkdir newiso
$ mv boot newiso
$ mkisofs -l -J -r -V TC-custom -no-emul-boot \
  -boot-load-size 4 \
  -boot-info-table -b boot/isolinux/isolinux.bin \
  -c boot/isolinux/boot.cat -o TC-remastered.iso newiso

# Optionally clean-up the temp dir
$ rm -rf newiso
```

Chapter 12. Remastering with a separate image

In order to better keep track of which files are modified or added, and to enable easier updating to a newer Core, it's recommended to use the method outlined in this chapter.

However, if you need to remove something from the image, for example to fit in tight memory constraints, this method will not work. It is only suitable for adding or changing files.

There are specific characteristics in the kernel's cpio loader that aren't present in the userspace utility: it allows you to load several images, either separately or concatenated together, and if the same file exists in more than one image, the later version overwrites the former.

This allows us to keep all our changes in a separate initrd image, making it easy to update to a newer Core version (literally only replacing core.gz and checking our modifications are up to date).

For the sake of an example, let's create a separate image that changes the login message.

12.1. Practice image

The login message is stored in **/etc/issue**. Therefore we need to create an image that contains the exact same path, with the contents we want to see.

```
$ cd /tmp
$ sudo mkdir -p ex/etc
$ echo "I believe!" | sudo tee ex/etc/issue
```

Now our new directory tree should look like this:

```
ex/
`-- etc/
    `-- issue

1 directory, 1 file
```

Let's pack it up like we would a normal remaster.

```
$ cd /tmp/ex
$ sudo find | sudo cpio -o -H newc | \
  gzip 2 > ../myimg.gz
$ advdef -z4 ../myimg.gz
```

To see whether the image works, boot it as outlined in the next section, and log out. Your new login text should be visible above the login prompt.

12.2. Booting with more than one initrd

Many bootloaders allow you to submit more than one image separately. For example, the syslinux family uses this syntax:

```
initrd=/boot/core.gz,/boot/myimg.gz
```

That is, you have the new image in the same directory as the main image, and place it after the original one, separated by a comma.

If using a bootloader that only supports one initrd (GRUB legacy, some of the DOS-based loaders, etc), you will need to cat the images together. This process is not easily reversible in userspace, so keep a separated copy of your new image around to do updates with.

```
$ cat core.gz myimg.gz > new.gz
```

Chapter 13. Including extensions in the ISO

This chapter will introduce the method of including extensions in an ISO image.

The Tiny Core and Core Plus ISOs are examples of this method - a bare Core plus extensions on the disc.

Since a CD is read-only, most of the operations you can perform on a normal **tce** directory cannot be done. For this reason, the directory is renamed **cde** when included in an ISO image.

The specifics of directory structure are exactly the same as for the **tce** directory.

13.1. Example: including nano

Since this example involves downloading dependencies, it's easiest to do on Core itself. Install advcomp.tcz and mkisofs-tools.tcz for the required programs.

First, copy the contents of the source ISO image:

```
$ sudo mkdir /mnt/tmp
$ sudo mount TinyCore-current.iso /mnt/tmp -o loop,ro
$ cp -a /mnt/tmp /tmp/newiso
$ sudo umount /mnt/tmp
```

Download nano into your **tce** directory:

```
$ tce-load -w nano
```

Copy nano and its dependencies to the **cde** directory, to be placed in the new ISO image:

```
$ cd /etc/sysconfig/tcedir/optional
$ tce-fetch nano.tcz.tree
$ for file in `cat nano.tcz.tree`; do
$       cp ${file}* /tmp/newiso/cde/optional
$ done

# Add it to onboot.lst, so it gets installed on boot.
$ echo nano.tcz >> /tmp/newiso/cde/onboot.lst
```

Create the ISO image, ready to be burned or booted in a virtual machine:

```
$ cd /tmp
$ mkisofs -l -J -r -V TC-custom -no-emul-boot \
  -boot-load-size 4 \
  -boot-info-table -b boot/isolinux/isolinux.bin \
  -c boot/isolinux/boot.cat -o TC-remastered.iso newiso
$ rm -rf newiso
```

When you boot this new ISO image, the nano editor will be available for use (installed on boot from the image).

In the above example, nano is mounted from the CD, meaning you can't eject the CD while running. The normal mechanism for loading the extensions to RAM can be used if this is desired: create an empty file called **copy2fs.flg** in the **cde** directory.

Chapter 14. Creating a personal (data) extension

When you have a set of unchanging data that needs to be stored outside your home directory, it's recommended to create an extension out of it rather than add it to the backup (where it would add to your boot and shutdown times).

The extension completely mirrors the resulting file system tree, so that if we want to see **/usr/share/mydir**, our extension should contain **usr/share/mydir**.

For an example, say you downloaded an icon theme from **gnome-look.org**. Icon themes should be installed to **/usr/share/icons/name** for a system-wide installation. It's a great example of this type of data: unchanging, and needs to be outside the home directory.

First, we'll create the tree we want to see inside the extension, in a temporary directory. We'll do this as root, so that system directories get the proper permissions and ownership.

```
$ sudo su
$ cd /tmp
$ mkdir myextension
$ cd myextension
$ mkdir -p usr/share/icons
```

Then, assuming the icon theme was unpacked to /tmp/gold (containing **/tmp/gold/16x16** and other icon directories), move it to the proper place:

```
$ sudo su # Still as root
$ mv /tmp/gold /tmp/myextension/usr/share/icons
```

Now we're ready to create an extension out of this directory tree. If you haven't already loaded the **squashfs-tools-4.x.tcz** extension, do so now.

```
$ cd /tmp
$ mksquashfs myextension myicons.tcz
```

 Our mksquashfs has been changed to use custom
defaults. If using a mksquashfs binary from elsewhere,
you need to add the options **-b 4k -no-xattrs** for the
same result.

Your personal extension is now ready. All it takes now is to move
it to your **tce** directory, and to set it as OnBoot (if you need it every
boot).

```
$ cd /tmp
$ mv -v myicons.tcz /etc/sysconfig/tcedir/optional

# Adding it to onboot.lst. Skip if you want it
# OnDemand or not in any list at all
# (manual loading only)
$ cd /etc/sysconfig/tcedir
$ echo myicons.tcz >> onboot.lst
```

You can install it right now with **tce-load -i myicons**, or you can
reboot to test whether it gets properly loaded on boot. Once the
extension is loaded, you should see the icons in **/usr/share/icons**,
and be able to use them in apps.

Chapter 15. Creating an extension

Creating an extension with binaries is no different from one containing mere data, like in the previous chapter. This chapter will mainly focus on the specifics of binaries, following the process from compiling to organizing them according to conventions.

By way of example, we'll be compiling **less**, a command-line document viewer. The process is no different for graphical applications, no actions are needed to make them have proper icons or menu items. Core follows the common FreeDesktop icon and menu standards.

To start, install the main development extension, **compiletc.tcz**. This meta-extension will install the GCC toolchain and system headers for you, corresponding to **build-essential** on Debian systems, and other names on other distributions.

15.1. Building less

Less uses the common Autotools build framework: "./configure && make && make install". Other build systems (cmake, custom makefiles, and so on) will require different steps; consult the program's install documentation if unsure.

As less needs ncurses to build, install it and its headers, **ncurses-dev.tcz**. We assume you have the latest less source downloaded and unpacked to /tmp.

 At this point, you would set the environment variables CFLAGS, CXXFLAGS and LDFLAGS. These variables affect the compiler and linker optimization, and vary by the target.

If building an extension for yourself, you may use any values; if building for the repository, see the wiki for the latest recommended values for your architecture. It's OK to leave them empty for your own extensions.

```
$ cd /tmp
$ cd less-458 # Latest version at the time

# Check the default options are OK
$ ./configure --help | more

# They are OK for less. Go with the defaults.
$ ./configure

# The process should run without errors.
# If not, google for the error message.
#
# Next, build less:
$ make
```

15.2. Creating the extension directory tree

While still in the less-458 directory, we'll use the Autotools support for installing to a destination directory, not to the running system (which would be lost on reboot).

```
# Again as root, so that system directory
# permissions and ownership is correct.
$ sudo make DESTDIR=/tmp/destless install
```

Taking a look in this temporary directory, the tree looks like this:

```
usr/
`-- local/
    |-- bin/
    |    |-- less*
    |    |-- lessecho*
    |    `-- lesskey*
    `-- share/
        `-- man/
            `-- man1/
                |-- less.1
                |-- lessecho.1
                `-- lesskey.1

6 directories, 6 files
```

We see that less installed three binaries, and three manual pages, all in the proper locations. As network access is quite common, it's conventional to remove manual pages and other documentation from extensions, or to have them in a separate -doc extension, so that the main extension can be smaller.

In this case, let's remove the man pages:

```
$ cd /tmp/destless
$ sudo rm -rf usr/local/share
```

It's also recommended to remove debugging symbols from the binaries, likewise for smaller size:

```
$ cd /tmp/destless/usr/local/bin
$ sudo strip -g *
```

15.3. Packing up

Creating a squashfs archive from the ready-made directory tree is the same as with a data-only extension: one simple invocation.

```
$ cd /tmp
$ mksquashfs destless myless.tcz
```

Chapter 16. Extension install scripts

Extensions may optionally include a script to be run after they're loaded. This is often used to make a default configuration file writable, or to work around some application that doesn't recognize its plugins if they are symlinks instead of real files.

These install scripts live in the **/usr/local/tce.installed** directory. They are named after the extension's file name, so for **myext-foo.tcz** the install script needs to be named **myext-foo**.

Install scripts run as root.

The install scripts should be owned by **tc:staff** and have executable permissions. The **tce.installed** directory should be owned by **root:staff** and have **775** permissions.

 Faulty permissions for the **tce.installed** directory may break extension loading.

16.1. Example: nano

For an example, let's take a look at what kind of install script would be needed for the nano editor.

Nano ships with a system-wide default configuration file. If the user loads the nano extension to RAM, the file will be writable, and nothing needs to be done; but what about the other case, default mounting?

In that case, the file would be a symlink to a read-only file, not what we want. So in the install script, we need to detect if the configuration file is a symlink, and if so, copy the real file in its place.

As the install scripts are run before the backup is restored, we never overwrite any custom configuration the user has done.

```sh
#!/bin/sh

CONFDIR=/usr/local/etc

[ -h $CONFDIR/nanorc ] && \
        rm -f $CONFDIR/nanorc && \
        cp -a /tmp/tcloop/nano/$CONFDIR/nanorc \
                $CONFDIR

# If the config file is a symlink,
# remove it, and copy the real file
# in its place.
#
# This is a no-op on copy2fs installs.
```

Chapter 17. Creating custom boot codes

Often it can be useful to set up custom boot codes to handle different cases. For example, a rescue USB stick might have a boot menu with several options: text boot, GUI boot, stress test...

The contents of the boot command line are visible in **/proc/cmdline**. Our shell functions collection, **tc-functions**, contains helper functions you can use in your scripts.

Example script, perhaps called from user **tc**'s **.profile**:

```
#!/bin/sh
# Include the helper functions
. /etc/init.d/tc-functions

# checkbootparam checks for the presence
# getbootparam gets the argument from "param=arg"
if $(checkbootparam stress); then
        type=$(getbootparam stresstype)

        case $type in
                cpu)
                        # CPU testing here
                ;;
                ram)
                        # RAM testing
                ;;
                *)
                        echo Unknown test $type
                        sleep 20
                ;;
        esac
fi
```

If the boot code "stress" is present, the script checks another boot code, "stresstype=foo", for which type of stress test to run.

This is a slightly contrived example to show the likely flow control.

In a real-life stress test bootcode, you wouldn't waste space by using two separate boot codes for the same thing, but instead would check for the presence of the same boot code.

If using **isolinux** with gfxboot, the boot menu might look like this:

Part III. Core internals

Chapter 18. The TCZ format

If one had to put it in a single sentence, TCZ could be described as "a loop-mounted squashfs 4.x archive, with specified parameters, usually symlinked into the main file system".

 With a mounted archive, we get to keep the bulk on the storage media, compressed and read-only (safe from the usual methods of corruption). Contrasting this to the majority of distros, which unpack the files but usually can't detect a change or corruption in a file, the TCZ method is more fail-safe.

That however only scratches the surface. In this chapter, we'll be looking to the design decisions behind it, and the gory details to its inner workings. The accompanying files are covered elsewhere; we shall only focus on TCZ here.

Starting from the installation method, the archive can either be mounted and symlinked, or its contents can be copied to the file system (usually RAM) for faster execution. The mount-and-symlink method is necessary in order to get the files in expected locations, while still keeping the data compressed and on the storage media, not extracted in RAM. The default is to mount.

It's often questioned why Core eschews the many union file systems, unlike most other live distributions. The reason for that is twofold: first, they tend to be unstable (buggy). There are quite a lot of mysterious crashes, and worse, disappearing files reported on the 'net for the various union file systems. Secondly, the system requirements for such a setup are higher. It would require more RAM to store the setup, and it would have more overhead per file access.

Why squashfs then, one might ask? The various mountable formats were compared in the earlier days, during the 1.x and 2.x time frame. Here are the various pros and cons:

Cramfs

* limited capacity, no time stamps, limited uid support

* supported in kernel

Zisofs

* a minimum size of 512KB - overhead for many smaller extensions

* supported in kernel

Mounting tar/zip archives via FUSE

* the overhead of FUSE

Squashfs came with full support for file attributes, good compression, and fully in-kernel support with good performance. After a few tries it was an easy decision.

18.1. Squashfs parameters

At the time, only gzip compression was supported, but since then the new options of LZO and XZ have been evaluated.

LZO created slightly bigger extensions, but its speed advantage was not seen in our use - the CPU could keep up fine with gzip compression, bottle-necked by the hard drive reading speed.

XZ, while nicely improving the compression ratio, comes with the downsides of LZMA: for each extension, it needs to keep the full dictionary in RAM. This means up to 1 MB extra RAM use per extension, depending on the exact settings used when creating the extension. The decompression was also measurably slower compared to gzip, no longer being able to be masked by the IO speed.

Therefore, our original decision to go with gzip compression for squashfs archives was still the correct one.

A run of similar tests was made to find the ideal block size for squashfs. While the larger blocks improved compression, squashfs keeps a few blocks cached in RAM per mount, so the compression had to be carefully balanced with the RAM requirement.

Unsurprisingly, the smallest block size, 4 KB, showed the best RAM behavior. The impact to compression and by proxy the reading speed was small enough, that this size was settled for. Current versions of Core refuse to load extensions created with other parameters.

18.2. What's inside?

The contents of a TCZ extension are nothing magic: it's the direct file system tree that can be found when you install an application or library. Let's take a look at lxterminal.tcz.

```
usr/local/bin/lxterminal
usr/local/share/applications/lxterminal.desktop
usr/local/share/lxterminal/lxterminal-preferences.ui
usr/local/share/lxterminal/lxterminal.conf
usr/local/share/pixmaps/lxterminal.png
```

It contains the main binary, lxterminal; the FreeDesktop standard .desktop file, specifying its icon and placement in any menus; the program's icon; and the program's private data. Nothing extra.

 The leading directories are there by necessity, but since they're uninteresting in this context, we skip them here.

This is what you would find under /tmp/somewhere after doing a "make install DESTDIR=/tmp/somewhere". Often documentation and development headers are further split to other extensions, for lower overhead to those who only want to use the extension.

Using the regular paths, with writable directories, means that most applications "just work".

There's power in simplicity.

Chapter 19. The boot process

At the high level, common distros' boot process consists of two parts: the initial RAM disk loads the storage drivers and finds the disk where the rest is stored; then the file system on the disk takes over, loading your services and applications.

Core is different, in that it never leaves the first stage. We fully run in the initial RAM disk, never leaving for a spinning disk (or a network mount, etc). There are other methods of "running in RAM" too, such as those used by Puppy, Knoppix, and DSL, which all do a variation of the usual method - they create a new, bigger RAM area, and move to it, letting the new part finish the boot.

 While the newer technology is called initial RAM FS (initramfs), not initial RAM disk (initrd), the terms will be used interchangeably here, always referring to the newer method.

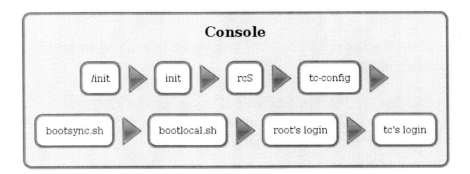

19.1. The first step: /init

Once the kernel has booted itself and unpacked our initramfs archive, it hands off control to a specific file, /init. This can be any executable, in our case it is a short shell script.

The tasks given for this very first program are only those not doable later as easily. It changes the allocated RAM space for /, optionally changing some options for **init** (a different program), and if a fallback setup is desired, does an old-style move of allocating new RAM space, copying the data there, and moving to it.

As this 16-line script finishes, it gives off control to the real init. This is the program that controls boot, shutdown, and reboot. It's the one that takes care of all your dead zombies, and listens for the user's ctrl-alt-del key-presses. It sets up the number of terminals requested, and fires up a login prompt program on each. Common options here are SysVinit, upstart, systemd, and busybox init. Core uses busybox init.

19.2. Real Boot: init

Busybox init is a BSD-style one, meaning it does not have runlevels, but runs one script on boot. At this point it does very little, giving control to our main boot script, tc-config (via rcS).

19.3. Bootstrap: rcS

The rcS script sets up some system mount points, and passes control to tc-config.

The first few initialization lines of tc-config were separated into rcS, to ease remaster maintenance. As one example, the Plymouth boot splash can be started from there.

19.4. Main boot: tc-config

The tc-config boot script is responsible for bringing up your hardware, acting on most boot codes, and making it possible for extensions to be loaded.

The order of events inside this script:

1. Check boot options

2. Fire up udev, start cold-plugging devices

3. Wait for slow USB devices if requested

4. Setup compressed swap in RAM, unless requested not to

5. Scan the available partitions, and create /etc/fstab with the results

6. Start up the system logger if requested

7. Setup language, timezone, clock, and hostname

8. Setup the requested username

9. If an extension server was requested over AoE, NBD, NFS, TFTP, or HTTP, handle it

10. If a virtual (loop) drive was requested, mount it

11. Setup persistent home and/or opt, if requested

12. Load laptop modules if requested

13. Enable swap if possible

14. Fire up extension loading

15. Fire up backup restore

16. Start bootsync.sh

After this sequence of events, the control moves to traditional userspace.

19.5. Bootsync.sh

This is the entry point for all items you need to run on boot, while the boot waits for them to complete. If you need network access later, this might be a good place to wait for the network to come up.

This script launches bootlocal.sh, backgrounded.

19.6. Bootlocal.sh

This is the entry point for all items that don't need to be waited for. This may include loading some non-essential module (ISA sound cards, for example), or starting some server.

19.7. Root's login

Once bootsync.sh is complete (and while bootlocal.sh happily does its own thing in the background, on another CPU core if there is one), init regains control.

As the boot is now complete from init's point of view, it feels safe to launch up all requested terminals. By default, this is only the first terminal, but with the **multivt** bootcode, you can request six.

The first terminal is configured to do an automatic login to root, only once. If you log out, this terminal will present a login prompt.

Root's login script is setup to do one of two things: if automatic login was disabled, it logs out, and otherwise, it passes the control up to our regular user, named **tc** by default.

19.8. Regular user

Now we're more in the regular distro territory: the normal user's login script does nothing out of the ordinary. If an X server is available, and a text-only boot was not requested, X is started.

19.9. The X Window System

The shipped .xsession file sets up the default background, starts any X-dependant programs you've configured, and starts up the configured window manager.

These parts only apply if you have the GUI extensions loaded (Xlibs, Xprogs, an X server, and a window manager). A command-line-only boot ends at user tc's login.

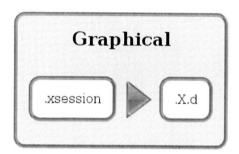

19.10. .X.d

This is the final part of the boot process. After starting up the window manager, the .xsession script sources and executes every file found in this directory (~/.X.d).

This is used to start up any programs that need X to run. For example, if you want to start a browser automatically on every boot, this is your location.

Chapter 20. The tce directory structure

Looking inside the **tce** directory, there are a variety of files: control files in plain text, and extensions as compressed archives. In this chapter we'll introduce the meaning and format of these control files.

Here's a typical **tce** directory:

```
.:
firstrun
onboot.lst
ondemand/
optional/
xwbar.lst

./ondemand:
ace-of-penguins

./optional:
ace-of-penguins.tcz
ace-of-penguins.tcz.md5.txt
nano.tcz
nano.tcz.dep
nano.tcz.md5.txt
ncurses-common.tcz
ncurses-common.tcz.md5.txt
ncurses.tcz
ncurses.tcz.dep
ncurses.tcz.md5.txt
upgrade/

./optional/upgrade:
ncurses.tcz
ncurses.tcz.dep
ncurses.tcz.md5.txt
```

Starting from the top level, we have two directories: **ondemand/** for the ondemand scripts (they install the extension, and optionally launch the program if one could be identified), and **optional/** for keeping the extensions.

The **optional/upgrade/** is a temporary directory, meaning these extension updates were downloaded this session, and will be applied on reboot.

This leaves us with the top-level plain text files.

20.1. Firstrun

This is an empty marker, whose existence means that the first-run dialog has been run and shouldn't be run again. The first-run dialog is run on the launch of **Apps**, asking whether you'd like to automatically choose the best mirror available.

The mirror chooser utility can be later on launched from the menu, if needed.

20.2. Onboot.lst

This is the plain text file containing a list of all extensions that should be loaded on boot. The files should be listed without paths, and are looked for only in the **optional/** directory.

This file may be managed via **Apps** or via your favorite text editor.

Example onboot.lst file:

```
nano.tcz
ace-of-penguins.tcz
```

20.3. Xwbar.lst

This file is formatted according to the **wbar** config file format. It lists the blocks that should not be included in **wbar**, the zooming quick-launch bar included by default.

Due to the format, it's preferred to edit this file via the **tc-wbarconf** utility, but hand-crafted edits are possible.

Example xwbar.lst file:

```
i: /usr/local/share/pixmaps/exit.png
t: Exit
c: exec exittc
```

20.4. Ondemand scripts

If you install an extension as OnDemand, a script will be generated for it under the **ondemand/** directory. If the extension can be detected as containing a single program, the script will also launch the program; if not, it will merely load the extension when called.

If the extension is detected as containing a single icon for the single program, this icon will copied to the **ondemand/** directory, and will be shown in **wbar** just like if the program were installed on boot. Upon clicking this icon, the generated script is called, and the icon is removed, replaced by the application's real icon.

These scripts are included in the window manager's menu whether or not they contain an icon or a program.

Example ondemand script:

```
#!/bin/sh
ondemand -e nano.tcz
```

Chapter 21. Accompanying extension files

Alongside a typical extension there are a set of meta-data files. Unlike the popular deb and rpm formats, the meta-data is not kept inside the archive itself. This allows meta-data updates without changing the main archive, which may be several hundred megabytes large.

While extension updates do take advantage of delta downloads via the **zsync** program, the amount of data transferred would still be several times larger if the meta-data were included in the main extension archive.

The accompanying files are:

• dep: direct dependencies

• info: size, license, author, updates, and usage information

• list: file list

• md5.txt: checksum

• tree: recursive list of dependencies

• zsync: used for delta updates

21.1. Dep files

These are plain text files listing the direct dependencies for the extension. As dependency resolution is recursive, these extensions may have dependencies of their own, and so the **.dep** files are usually quite small.

nano.tcz.dep:

```
ncurses.tcz
```

21.2. Info files

Modeled after the .lsm format used in old software archives, the info file identifies the extension and its main properties: size, description, creator, license, and so on.

Often the comments field includes usage instructions specific to Core, and the change-log field may include required actions for the update, so it's advised to read the info file for any extension you install/update.

nano.tcz.info:

```
Title:            nano.tcz
Description:      Nano editor
Version:          2.2.6
Author:           Various
Original-site:    http://www.nano-editor.org/
Copying-policy:   GPL
Size:             88K
Extension_by:     Curaga
Tags:             Nano editor
Comments:         The most essential component of any
                  unix system, and my personal favourite
                  editor: Nano!

                  Has most advanced options enabled,
                  color syntax highlighting, multibuffer,
                  suspend etc.

Change-log:       2008/07/05 - First version
                  2008/12/09 - Update to 2.0.9,
                               this time in /usr/local
                  2009/10/05 - Removed user.tar.gz
Current:          2011/05/25 - Update to 2.2.6
```

21.3. List files

This is a free-form list of files included in the extension. It can be created using **find**, **unsquashfs**, or other tools.

nano.tcz.list:

```
usr/local/bin/nano
usr/local/bin/rnano
usr/local/etc/nanorc
usr/local/etc/nanorc.sample
usr/local/share/nano/asm.nanorc
usr/local/share/nano/c.nanorc
usr/local/share/nano/groff.nanorc
usr/local/share/nano/html.nanorc
usr/local/share/nano/java.nanorc
usr/local/share/nano/man.nanorc
usr/local/share/nano/mutt.nanorc
usr/local/share/nano/nanorc.nanorc
usr/local/share/nano/patch.nanorc
usr/local/share/nano/perl.nanorc
usr/local/share/nano/pov.nanorc
usr/local/share/nano/python.nanorc
usr/local/share/nano/ruby.nanorc
usr/local/share/nano/sh.nanorc
usr/local/share/nano/tex.nanorc
usr/local/tce.installed/nano
```

21.4. Md5 files

These are checksum files, obtained directly from the **md5sum** utility.

nano.tcz.md5.txt:

```
02e231701c2d272f81cda33f16eace11  nano.tcz
```

21.5. Tree files

These are files generated by the server, containing a flattened listing of all dependencies for the extension. They are available for convenience, and used for functions like the size tab in **Apps**, or for copying an extension and all its dependencies.

nano.tcz.tree:

```
nano.tcz
   ncurses.tcz
      ncurses-common.tcz
```

21.6. Zsync files

These are binary files generated by the **zsyncmake** utility. They are hosted server-side to enable delta downloads for faster, lower-bandwidth extension updates.

We also host zsync files for the main ISO images, enabling you to download newer versions rather quickly and cheaply.

Part IV. Projects

Chapter 22. Simple Web server

By Luiz Fernando Estevarengo AKA Zendrael

Building a simple web server is really easy with Core and Busybox HTTPD. This server is tiny and fast, although it does not run some server-side pages, you can run CGI scripts - you can even write a shell script to act like a CGI.

Install the busybox-httpd.tcz extension via Apps or by the command line, OnBoot so that it's loaded every time the computer boots up. To start it each boot, include this line in **/opt/bootlocal.sh**:

```
/usr/local/httpd/sbin/httpd -p 85 \
        -h /home/tc/public_html -u tc:staff
```

We're specifying that the server will run on port 85, will load files stored in the public_html folder under my user, and will run as the user **tc** with group **staff**. This is a conf-less method so you don't need a config file.

By default, Busybox-HTTPD doesn't list files in directories, it will always look for an index.html file. If you prefer to have a directory listing feature, you must add a CGI script for it, also provided by the extension:

```
$ mkdir -p /home/tc/public_html/cgi-bin
$ cp /usr/local/httpd/index.cgi \
        /home/tc/public_html/cgi-bin

# Make sure it has proper permissions
$ chmod 755 /home/tc/public_html/cgi-bin/index.cgi
```

A quick reboot later, it's ready to go, serving files over the web!

22.1. Custom CGI example

If you want to control the system via a web browser, or to read statistics for example, you can write custom CGI scripts in the shell.

Here's a hello world CGI shell script:

```
#!/bin/sh
echo -e "Content-type: text/html\r\n\r\n"
echo "<h1>Hello world!</h1>"
```

When placed in the **cgi-bin** directory, named as **hello.sh**, and given executable permission, you can point your browser to localhost/cgi-bin/hello.sh to test it.

Chapter 23. Automated network installer

In this chapter, we'll build a PXE-bootable image that partitions and formats the local disk, installs a bootloader, and unpacks a preset tarball to the new partition.

It may be used for quick mass installations, or booted from a CD/USB as a conventional automated installer.

What the image installs is not specified here; it need not be Core.

23.1. Start files

We need to download the kernel and main initrd, vmlinuz and core.gz, from any mirror. The installer logic will be placed in an additional initrd.

This procedure may be performed from any linux distribution; the downloaded extension has no dependencies, so it is easy to do with a web browser if necessary.

Download the syslinux extension:

```
$ tce-load -w syslinux
```

23.2. The installer script

We'll include an installer script in the new initrd, and call it from **bootsync.sh**, so that its output is visible on screen.

```
$ sudo su
# When editing the main system files, it's best to be
# root, so that permissions and ownership are correct.

$ cd /tmp
$ mkdir -p initrd/opt
$ cp /opt/bootsync.sh initrd/opt
$ editor initrd/opt/bootsync.sh
```

Add a call to your script to the end, making sure the network is up before starting it:

```
count=0
echo -n Waiting for the network...
while [ "$count" -lt 60 ]; do
        ifconfig eth0 | grep -q inet && break
        sleep 1
        count=$((count + 1))
        echo -n .
done

/opt/installer.sh
```

Create the installer script, marking it as executable:

```
$ sudo su
# When editing the main system files, it's best to be
# root, so that permissions and ownership are correct.

$ cd /tmp/initrd/opt
$ touch installer.sh
$ chmod a+x installer.sh
$ editor installer.sh
```

Here's the example contents:

```
#!/bin/sh

TARGET=/dev/sda

out() {
        sync; sync
        poweroff
}

# Check there is a disk
fdisk -l $TARGET 2>&1 | grep -q bytes
[ "$?" -ne 0 ] && echo "No disk found" && \
        sleep 10 && out

# Zero out the partition table
dd if=/dev/zero of=$TARGET bs=512 count=1

# Partition it to two
# Swap is set up at 256 Mb, rest for ext4
fdisk $TARGET << EOF
n
p
1

+256M
t
82
n
p
2


w
EOF

mkswap ${TARGET}1
mkfs.ext4 ${TARGET}2

cat /usr/local/share/syslinux/mbr.bin > $TARGET
```

```
# Mount it, grab the tarball
mkdir /mnt/target
mount ${TARGET}2 /mnt/target

cd /mnt/target
wget http://my-url.com/files.tgz
tar xvf files.tgz
rm files.tgz

# Install extlinux
mkdir -p boot/extlinux
extlinux -i /mnt/target/boot/extlinux

cd /
umount /mnt/target

# Done!
clear
echo Success.
sleep 5
out
```

We'll also need to unpack the syslinux extension to this new initrd.
To do this on Core, install the squashfs-tools-4.x extension.

```
$ sudo su
$ cd /tmp
$ unsquashfs syslinux.tcz
$ cp -a squashfs-root/* initrd
```

23.3. Packing up & testing

Let's pack our new initrd image up:

```
$ cd /tmp/initrd
$ sudo find | sudo cpio -o -H newc | \
  gzip 2 > ../myimg.gz
$ advdef -z4 ../myimg.gz
```

Try booting the new image in a virtual machine with a hard drive
attached - the whole process should be quite fast.

Chapter 24. Private cloud

Cloud is such a buzzword. It means everything and nothing.

For the purposes of this chapter, it means you set up an old computer at home, sharing your files, letting you access them from anywhere, including your phone.

Since file serving takes little CPU, any old clunker ought to be of use; if the power demands matter, we recommend re-purposing a thin client or a laptop, as they often use only 15-25W.

Most file sharing protocols are insecure; it's not recommended to expose SMB or NFS to the internet. We'll be setting up two servers: busybox httpd giving passworded read-only access to our files, and a SSH server giving secure read-write access.

We assume you have installed Core to the computer, and have persistence set up. For this example, we'll be sharing the files on **sda1/files**.

It's assumed there's a NAT router between the box and the internet; it will handle port forwarding and firewalling. It's assumed the data disk is the same as where Core is installed; otherwise, it needs to be mounted in **bootlocal.sh**.

24.1. SSH

For SSH, we have the choice of using dropbear, or the OpenSSH server. If SFTP is required, you'll need OpenSSH; for this example, we'll assume shell and scp are enough, and will pick dropbear. Install your selected SSH server extension, OnBoot.

For file access, we'll create a separate user that has no other rights. His home directory shall be the files directory.

```
$ sudo adduser -H -h /mnt/sda1/files johndoe
# -H: don't create directory
# -h: path to home directory

# We need to give our new user write access to files
$ sudo chown -R johndoe /mnt/sda1/files
```

To start dropbear on boot, add the following line to **/opt/bootlocal.sh**:

```
/etc/init.d/dropbear start
```

To save our new user, their password, and the SSH host keys, add these lines to the backup in **/opt/.filetool.lst**:

```
etc/passwd
etc/shadow
etc/group
etc/dropbear
```

Generate the host keys now, and run a backup:

```
$ sudo /etc/init.d/dropbear start
$ backup
```

24.2. HTTPD

There is a pre-compiled extension for busybox httpd, **busybox-httpd.tcz**. If you need to customize it, busybox is fairly easy to compile.

Start by creating the config file for it:

```
$ sudo su
$ echo "/:foo:bar" > /mnt/sda1/httpd.conf
```

This file disallows all access without the given username (foo) and password (bar).

To start it on boot, add the following to **/opt/bootlocal.sh**:

```
/usr/local/httpd/sbin/httpd -u nobody:nogroup \
        -r "Private." -c /mnt/sda1/httpd.conf \
        -h /mnt/sda1/files
```

As busybox httpd doesn't support file listings natively, it comes with a CGI program to do it instead. Copy it to the proper place:

```
$ mkdir /mnt/sda1/files/cgi-bin
$ cp /usr/local/httpd/index.cgi /mnt/sda1/files/cgi-bin

# Make sure it has proper permissions
$ chmod 755 /mnt/sda1/files/cgi-bin/index.cgi
```

24.3. Connections, ports

Many routers have a DynDNS (or other such service) client built-in. These services give you a DNS address even if your IP is not stable, as it often is not in home connections.

As your NAT router handles port forwarding, you get to decide which ports to redirect to your cloud's ports 22 (SSH) and 80 (HTTP). It's not recommended to use the port 22 publicly, as that's painting a target on your door - there are automated bots trying to attack every server with port 22 open. Even though using a non-standard SSH port is mere security by obscurity, it's not humans that move is intended to deter, but automatic bots and scripts.

For the HTTP port, most phones let you use a port other than 80, but using a port other than the common ones (80, 443, or 8080) may be blocked by some 3G networks.

24.4. Security considerations

HTTP and HTTP authentication is insecure. Anyone can snoop your username, password, and data - don't use a sensitive one for these credentials, or download sensitive files over the HTTP connection.

It's however a balance with usability. Most devices support HTTP and HTTP authentication; SSH access can be considered considerably more luxurious.

As the router is assumed to handle firewalling, no firewall is installed on the box in this example. Adding one would be an additional defense layer, but its advantage in practice would be small in this scenario.

Using a heavier HTTP server would allow SSL connections, giving slightly better protection for the read-only access. However SSH with public key authentication is recommended for sensitive data.

The HTTP server is run as nobody, without any kind of write access to the system. Along with the simplicity of busybox, it's unlikely for there to be a remote exploit for it. A chroot may be added on top to isolate the server from the core system; though the valuable data would be inside the chroot.

HTTP server logging would be available by adding the **-v -f** options to the start line, preventing the server from daemonizing and requesting verbose output. Redirecting stderr to a file would preserve the logs. Remember in this case to have the httpd server be the last line in bootlocal.sh, as the lines after it wouldn't execute.

24.5. Final result

You have your own personal cloud humming over there, giving you access to your data all over the world. Sharing subfolders with specific passwords, say holiday pictures to far-living family, is just one config change away.

Assuming your end-device allows it, you have secure upload, download and shell; otherwise, you have read-only HTTP access.

The required extensions + the CGI script total about 120kb of disk space. Both servers use about 500kb of RAM. The overhead over Core itself is small enough not to matter; if the computer has enough RAM to run a shell, it can run this scenario. A Pentium with 32mb of RAM would be adequate.

Chapter 25. A thin remote desktop client

In this chapter, we'll build an ISO image that automatically launches a RDP session to a pre-determined target.

Overview of steps:

1. Grab the latest TinyCore ISO (X is needed)

2. Add the rdesktop extension and dependencies to the ISO

3. Make the boot wait for getting an IP address

4. Fire up rdesktop when the system is up

To start with, download the latest TinyCore ISO from your closest mirror.

25.1. Add the rdesktop extension and dependencies to the ISO

In order to easily get the extensions we need, we'll be doing the remaster inside the fresh TinyCore ISO we just downloaded. Start it either in a virtual machine, or on real hardware.

With our environment up, download the rdesktop and gconv extensions:

```
$ tce-load -w rdesktop glibc_gconv
```

The gconv extension contains the data files for converting text between character sets; it's an optional dependency of rdesktop.

As we're running in the cloud mode, all extensions will be kept in RAM, in **/tmp/tce**. With a fresh image, only rdesktop and its dependencies will be there.

Let's mount and copy the ISO we booted from:

```
# The CD might already be mounted, but just in case:
$ sudo mount /dev/sr0
$ cp -a /mnt/sr0 /tmp/newiso
```

The copy might warn about not being able to keep the file ownership; this warning is harmless.

Copy rdesktop and its dependencies to the **cde** directory on the new ISO:

```
$ cd /tmp/tce/optional
$ sudo cp * /tmp/newiso/cde/optional

# Add it to onboot.lst, so it gets installed on boot.
$ chmod u+w /tmp/newiso/cde/onboot.lst
$ echo rdesktop.tcz >> /tmp/newiso/cde/onboot.lst
$ echo glibc_gconv.tcz >> /tmp/newiso/cde/onboot.lst
```

If you want to disable **wbar** in the new image, edit the new **onboot.lst** and remove the wbar.tcz line.

Now that the extensions have been copied, we can install the extensions needed to create the ISO:

```
$ tce-load -wi advcomp mkisofs-tools
```

25.2. Make the boot wait for getting an IP address

A normal Core boot does not wait for the network to be up; however, for a dedicated RDP client, that's what we want to happen.

To make the boot wait for it, we need to add the commands to one of the synchronous files. Since this is a system-wide resource we're waiting for, **/opt/bootsync.sh** is our target.

We'll include our customizations in a new initrd file:

```
$ sudo su
# When editing the main system files, it's best to be
# root, so that permissions and ownership are correct.

$ cd /tmp
$ mkdir -p initrd/opt
$ cp /opt/bootsync.sh initrd/opt
$ editor initrd/opt/bootsync.sh
```

Paste the following piece of script to the end of the file:

```
count=0
echo -n Waiting for the network...
while [ "$count" -lt 60 ]; do
        ifconfig eth0 | grep -q inet && break
        sleep 1
        count=$((count + 1))
        echo -n .
done
```

This piece of script will wait up to 60 seconds, checking if the first wired network card has an IP address, and if it does, breaking out of the loop.

25.3. Fire up rdesktop when the system is up

We'll add a file to the default user's **.X.d** directory. This script piece will run rdesktop in a loop, popping up an error message if it fails for some reason.

Given that no writable disk will be mounted, the system can be safely turned off via the physical power button. If this is to run on a set of dedicated terminals, it might also be useful to add a cron job to turn the system off at preset hours.

```
$ sudo su
# When editing the main system files, it's best to be
# root, so that permissions and ownership are correct.

$ cd /tmp/initrd
$ mkdir -p etc/skel/.X.d
$ cd etc/skel/.X.d
$ editor rdesktop
```

Add the desired rdesktop command line to the file:

```
while [ 1 ]; do
        rdesktop -u user 10.0.2.2:7777 2> /tmp/rderr
        [ "$?" -ne 0 ] && popup `cat /tmp/rderr`
done
```

This starts up rdesktop, directing errors to a file, and if the launch
fails, show the errors to the user with a popup message.

Let's pack our new initrd image up:

```
$ cd /tmp/initrd
$ sudo find | sudo cpio -o -H newc | \
  gzip 2 > ../myimg.gz
$ advdef -z4 ../myimg.gz
```

Let's place the initrd on the ISO, and have it be used:

```
$ cd /tmp/newiso/boot
$ sudo mv /tmp/myimg.gz .
$ sudo sed -i 's@core.gz@&,/boot/myimg.gz@g' \
  isolinux/isolinux.cfg
```

If you'd like to tweak the boot menu, or set other boot options, edit
isolinux.cfg now.

Finally, create the ISO image:

```
$ cd /tmp
$ sudo mkisofs -l -J -r -V TC-custom -no-emul-boot \
  -boot-load-size 4 \
  -boot-info-table -b boot/isolinux/isolinux.bin \
  -c boot/isolinux/boot.cat -o TC-remastered.iso newiso
```

25.4. Result

Our new ISO image boots gracefully to the desktop, waiting for the network to be up, running the RDP client in a loop.

Booting the image in KVM takes under one second.

The ISO image is approximately 17 Mb in size, and the system uses 35 Mb of RAM when running. It's recommended to add about 5-20 Mb to that to account for different resolutions and drivers, putting the required RAM for this image at 55 Mb (64 Mb rounded to the nearest common size).

Chapter 26. File hosting via FTP

Often you might need somebody to send you a bigger file, which is untenable over plain old e-mail. The common alternatives nowadays are third-party hosters such as Mega and Mediafire, or cloud services such as those from Microsoft, Google, or Dropbox.

The downside to these third-party services (besides the obvious reliance on a third party - if they go down, you can't get to your file) is that they're not compatible with all browsers, occasionally seemingly break at random, and sometimes host intrusive ads. They also cannot be automated easily, or require personal information to upload/download.

To this end, we'll be setting up a FTP server with anonymous uploads, and a read-only downloads section. FTP can be easily scripted, and it tends to be more efficient at serving files than HTTP.

Please keep in mind that FTP works over plain text; don't store confidential data here, or use any secure passwords for the authenticated content.

It's assumed the data drive is mounted on boot. We'll be using **sda1** in this example.

26.1. Installing & configuration

We'll be using a small server called BFTPD. Install **bftpd.tcz** onboot, and add this line to **/opt/bootlocal.sh**:

```
bftpd -d -c /mnt/sda1/bftpd.conf
```

Copy the supplied example config file to the drive, and open it in your favorite editor:

```
$ cp /usr/local/etc/bftpd.conf.sample \
       /mnt/sda1/bftpd.conf
$ editor /mnt/sda1/bftpd.conf
```

The entries we'll consider now are HELLO_STRING, QUIT_MSG
(cosmetic messages), the ALLOWCOMMAND ones, the
USERLIMIT ones, and the user sections.

Once the hello and quit messages are to your liking, check that
the only allowed command is STOR - users aren't allowed to
delete files, or to send site commands (special server-dependent
commands).

You might want to limit the connections with the USERLIMIT
variables, in particular USERLIMIT_SINGLEUSER that stops a
single user being logged in many times at once.

In the user section, the default file sets up the anonymous login as
redirecting to the system user **ftp**. This fits us well. However, we
want anonymous logins to be enabled, and the user to be restricted
to our data drive, so remove the DENY_LOGIN variable from the
user ftp section, making the section look like this:

```
user ftp {
  #Any password fits.
  ANONYMOUS_USER="yes"
  CHANGE_UID="yes"
}
```

The next steps are creating the **ftp** user, backing up the user files,
and creating the upload and download directories with appropriate
permissions.

```
$ sudo adduser -h /mnt/sda1 -D -H ftp
# Their home dir is /mnt/sda1,
# they don't have a password, and
# the directory will be created manually.

# Add the user files to the backup.
# This can also be done via the GUIs if desired.
$ echo "etc/passwd" >> /opt/.filetool.lst
$ echo "etc/shadow" >> /opt/.filetool.lst
$ echo "etc/group" >> /opt/.filetool.lst

$ cd /mnt/sda1
$ mkdir upload download
$ sudo chown ftp upload
$ chmod o-w download
$ sudo chmod g+w upload

# Anything placed in the download dir
# is read-only via FTP.
```

As a sanity check before rebooting, start the server in no-fork mode to see that there are no typos in the config file, or other issues:

```
$ sudo bftpd -D -c /mnt/sda1/bftpd.conf
# If there are no errors, press ctrl-C
```

26.2. Testing

After a reboot, our FTP server should be running. Check that it's present in the running processes list by running **ps**, and that it's listening by running **netstat -l -t**.

A command-line FTP client is available in the **inetutils** extension, but you can use any browser or FTP client to test the uploads and downloads.

26.3. Results

You now have a convenient place to store files from anywhere. The server requires about 500kb of RAM per logged-in user.

Chapter 27. Network booting

Core can easily be booted via the network (PXE). This may be used to have many diskless computers, for example as stand-alone web browser stations, or as thin clients that rely on the server for some needs; or as a distribution method for an installer, recovery setup, or anything else you can come up with.

Core is also capable of being the boot server, but it's not required; you may use any system with TFTP, PXE (DHCP), and HTTP/NFS/ other file sharing protocol as the server, from CentOS to Debian to even Windows. We don't recommend that last option though.

Core includes a quick setup wizard for testing PXE booting, **tc-terminal-server**. It allows you to quickly setup one machine as a mothership, sharing the base image, to test if the other computers on your network (and the network itself) work for PXE booting. For more permanent setups, it's not recommended to use the wizard.

As the server setups vary wildly, we won't go into the configuration details of any specific one in this chapter. Instead we cover the available options, helping you decide which setup fits your needs the best.

Steps

a. Selecting the base image

b. Are separate extensions needed?

c. Other considerations

27.1. Selecting the base image

For thin clients, the obvious option is to use the shipped image, the
normal **core.gz** and kernel. However, if the clients are to be stand-
alone, it might make sense to create a remaster instead, holding
your modifications in a second initrd (pxelinux is capable of using
multiple initrds).

The constraints of the clients also factor in. If they are low in RAM,
a remaster where everything is in RAM may prove unfeasible;
in this situation, you may trade performance for lower RAM use
by mounting extensions from the server. It does increase network
demands, but as the extensions are then not copied to client RAM,
only cached in the file system cache, it can save a lot of RAM.

27.2. Are separate extensions needed?

If the extensions are integrated into the initrd, as in the above
section, then you can skip this section.

Core supports several ways of loading extensions over the network.
Some of these (NFS, NBD, AOE) mount the share over the network,
using the extensions remotely from the server; the others (TFTP,
HTTP) download the extensions over the given protocol to RAM,
then mount them from there.

Considering the latter option, one might ask what's the difference
to just having them in the initrd in the first place. After all, in both
cases they are downloaded from the server into the client's RAM.
The difference is in boot speed: TFTP, even when tuned to use high
block sizes, is a slow protocol - using HTTP may improve transfer
speeds greatly.

The other part is the more even access pattern: if everything were in
one initrd, that client would make one big request; if each extension
was requested individually, the network requests would be more
spread out over time.

One may also combine the mount-a-share approaches with having extensions OnDemand. This combination would allow for very quick boot speeds, and less network usage, as the bigger applications would only be requested once the user starts them.

 You're not limited to the mentioned protocols. If there's a Linux client for your file protocol, you can include just that client and the extension downloading logic in the initrd, allowing you to use more exotic protocols to download or mount extensions from the server.

27.3. Other considerations

The extensions are usually read-only from the clients' end, making it easy to upgrade in one place, at the server, and a reboot of the client is all that's needed. Often some data needs to be RW though, perhaps home directories over NFS, perhaps some other shared folder for common data.

The memory use needs to be considered. A diskless client may have little recourse when its RAM runs out. While Core ships the **zram** module by default, allowing you to over-commit the RAM by about 20%, you may still need swap.

Swapping over the network is not advised; it's not yet quite stable in the current kernels, and doing it over the network may cause too much congestion. As a backup, you might consider letting the clients have HDDs, but only as swap partitions.

Chapter 28. Bringing up old hardware - common gotchas

Older hardware often carries limitations. This chapter lists some of them, and what you can do about them.

One might question the point in doing so, particularly if electricity costs in the area are high. However, getting some use of old hardware can be fruitful, often free of any immediate costs, and helps reduce electronic waste.

The power use of old computers is not high in comparison to modern desktop computers, so if you have a job they can perform, the power costs may not create a big enough offset to pay for a new computer.

The power usage of old computers is surprisingly low compared to modern 500W power guzzlers; a first-generation Pentium may run in 60W full, less than the new power guzzler runs at idle.

28.1. BIOS

The firmware, most often buggy, and coincidentally, most often not user-replaceable beyond flashing an image from the manufacturer, may carry a number of limitations.

Even if claiming to support a boot method (USB, CD, PXE, floppy), that support might be buggy. BIOSes from the USB 1 era will often only boot from USB with the USB-ZIP emulation mode.

Should the BIOS not support booting from a CD, and a PXE setup is inconvenient, we recommend removing the hard disk, and installing to it on another computer. Core does not read any info from the installing computer, so the resulting install will work just fine when moved to the target. Alternatively, Smart Boot Manager may be used to chain-load the CD from the floppy drive.

If the target has integrated graphics, the BIOS often controls the amount of RAM to assign to the graphics card. This amount limits the resolutions you can use, and the acceleration that can be available. If you have the choice, use a minimum of 16 MB.

Some BIOSes, notably Dell ones with Intel graphics, either don't offer that choice, or only offer very small choices. On these machines the only way around the limit is to use Xorg with the fully accelerated driver, as it can control the RAM allocation regardless of the BIOS. With Xvesa or the framebuffer, you might be limited to 640x480 at a low color depth.

28.2. Sound

Core offers two sound systems: ALSA and OSS. OSS doesn't support any ISA cards, so if the sound card is connected via the ISA bus (either as an extension card, or by an integrated ISA bus on the motherboard), your only choice is ALSA.

ISA sound cards often cannot be automatically detected. In these cases, you will need to find out the name of the sound module, and to add a modprobe call to **bootlocal.sh**. Often you might need to also pass the card's parameters (IRQ, DMA address) as options to the driver module.

28.3. VESA support

Some older graphics cards don't have proper support for the VESA standard. This means that the standard Xvesa server might display at a wrong resolution, with wrong colors, or fail to start altogether.

In these cases, the options are the framebuffer, and Xorg. To use a framebuffer resolution, you need to add the **vga=791** bootcode to your bootloader's config file (where 791 is a number specifying the resolution and color depth - this particular one is 1024x768 at 16bit color depth), and to install the Xfbdev server instead of Xvesa.

Table of common VESA resolutions:

	640x480	800x600	1024x768	1280x1024
256 colors	769	771	773	775
16-bit	785	788	791	794
24-bit	786	789	792	795

Should the framebuffer also fail, or if non-VESA resolutions are needed, you'll need to install Xorg with a suitable driver.

 There doesn't exist a Xorg driver for all cards - check online before trying.

28.4. Networking

ISA network cards have the same downsides as ISA sound cards: you may need to manually modprobe the correct driver, and to pass the card's details as driver parameters.

PCMCIA network cards should work automatically, as long as the PCMCIA bus itself is recognized. You can use the **lspcmcia** command to list any attached cards to see if they are recognized.

Should the computer not have a network card, Linux supports various other ways to move data in addition to plain old ethernet. You can harness infrared, the serial or parallel port, or even the sound card to move data (yes, even to browse the internet!) as long as you have another computer that can act as a router.

28.5. Bigger hard drives

The IDE bus will usually accept drives as large as you can buy, up to terabytes, even on computers that were sold with 10 GB drives. The possible issue with these is that the BIOS cannot read past a certain size, even though Linux can.

The solution to this issue is to create a separate boot partition at the beginning of the disk, making sure the BIOS can read all of it. The common BIOS limits are 137 GB, 8.5 GB, and 528 MB, so by making your boot partition be less than 500 MB in size you guarantee that the BIOS will be able to read it.

For Core, the boot partition only needs to contain the boot loader, kernel, and **core.gz**. Any personal data and extensions can reside on different partitions.

28.6. Memory limitations

Of all the limits, RAM might be the hardest to overcome. While used RAM sticks of the older technologies can be bought for cheap, the computer may not be able to take much (each motherboard has a maximum amount). A large swap partition is recommended (at least 100 MB).

As long as there's enough RAM to boot Core itself (28 MB in text mode, 48 MB in GUI at the time of writing), a lot can be done through selecting lightweight programs. Instead of the latest Firefox or Chrome, consider an older version of Opera; if Javascript support is not needed, Dillo; if text is enough, lynx or links.

 Some versions of Links can display images. It is a very lightweight browser if the features are enough.

Likewise, for playing music, eschew the complex GUI players like Amarok in favor of simpler ones like XMMS, or command-line ones like mpg123 or mplayer.

To write documents, Ted is a lightweight RTF editor. Older OpenOffice may be considered for more complex documents.

Should the target not have enough RAM to run Core itself, there are some things you can do to help the situation with a remaster. The base image contains a couple megabytes of drivers: by removing those the target doesn't need, you can lower the required RAM. Using text mode is a given.

Depending on the situation, **zram** may or may not be useful. With very little RAM, the compressed swap in RAM might actually act counter-intuitively, not leaving enough to run the desired program, causing constant swapping. You can disable it with the bootcode **nozswap**.

Chapter 29. A Web kiosk

By Luiz Fernando Estevarengo AKA Zendrael

A kiosk machine is essentially a terminal to access the web: any website, just one website, or perhaps a web app. It does not run any kind of app other than the web browser.

With Core, we can build a simple kiosk with little effort, a bunch of extensions and the creation of an add-on to our browser of choice.

We assume persistent home/opt are not used, and that the home dir is under backup. This enables a clean slate on each reboot.

29.1. Selecting extensions

Starting with an installed TinyCore, you will need:

- **firefox.tcz** (our browser)

- **idesk.tcz** (for the screen icons)

- **liberation-fonts-ttf.tcz** (many sites are designed for Microsoft fonts)

- **openbox.tcz** (deals better with our add-on later)

Load all these extensions OnBoot.

If you want to let the user do more on the web, you can also use **alsa.tcz**, **getflash.tcz**, and your choice of Firefox add-ons.

For a better looking experience, you may want to have a gtk2 theme engine loaded with a theme of your choice. This will not be covered as it depends on your preferences.

29.2. Configuring Core extensions

29.2.1. iDesk icons

What happens if our user, for some reason, closes the browser
or it crashes? We must have an easy way to restart the browser,
preferably with a visual clue, like an icon in the desktop. iDesk lets
us do this with icons that can not be changed, deleted or moved on
the desktop.

 You may also choose to use the included **wbar**; or to
not have icons at all, but to run Firefox in a loop (so that
when the previous instance closes, a new one is started).

Inside your home directory create one file, **.ideskrc** which will
contain the iDesk configuration; and one directory, where your
icons will be kept, **.idesktop**:

```
$ touch .ideskrc
$ mkdir .idesktop
$ editor .ideskrc
```

Edit the **.ideskrc** config file to reflect the colors of your desktop and
some grid options:

```
table Config
    FontName: sans
    FontSize: 10
    FontColor: #ffffff
    Locked: false
    Transparency: 50
    Shadow: true
    ShadowColor: #000000
    ShadowX: 1
    ShadowY: 2
    Bold: false
    ClickDelay: 100
    IconSnap: true
    SnapWidth: 55
    SnapHeight: 100
    SnapOrigin: BottomRight
    SnapShadow: true
    SnapShadowTrans: 200
    CaptionOnHover: false
end
table Actions
    Lock: control right doubleClk
    Reload: middle doubleClk
    Drag: false
    EndDrag: left singleClk
    Execute[0]: left doubleClk
    Execute[1]: right doubleClk
end
```

Now, inside the **.idesktop** directory we will create the file that contains the information of our icon, to restart the browser should it crash or should the user close it:

```
$ cd .idesktop
$ touch kiosk.lnk
$ editor kiosk.lnk
```

With this content:

```
table Icon
    Caption: Web
    Icon: .idesktop/web.png
    X: 100
    Y: 100
    Command[0]: firefox
end
```

Note the icon mentioned in the .idesktop folder. You can use any icon you want; to use the Firefox icon, you can copy it from **/usr/local/share/pixmaps**.

29.2.2. iDesk autoload

As iDesk will serve to show an icon for our browser, we need to start it in a suitable place. So, in the **~/.X.d/** directory we will create a file to start it up:

```
$ mkdir -p ~/.X.d
$ cd ~/.X.d
$ echo "idesk &" > idesk
```

29.2.3. Firefox profile

We will create a custom profile to handle the kiosk. Open and close Firefox at least once so that the default profile gets created.

Open up a terminal and type:

```
$ cd ~/.mozilla/firefox
$ ls
```

You will find a directory like **j08765.default** and a file named **profiles.ini**. We will change the profile name to a more convenient one, and set it in the ini file:

```
$ mv *.default kiosk.default
$ editor profiles.ini
```

Then change the Path in profiles.ini to kiosk.default as follows:

```
[General]
StartWithLastProfile=1

[Profile0]
Name=kiosk
IsRelative=1
Path=kiosk.default
```

Start and close Firefox to see that the moved profile is working.

29.2.4. Firefox autoload

We will need to have Firefox loaded as soon as our kiosk runs X.
Here we follow the same way that we used for idesk:

```
$ cd ~/.X.d
$ echo "firefox &" > firefox
```

29.2.5. Configuring Firefox

To make the best of our kiosk, we will setup it to use less space on
the screen, and avoid some troubles with ads. Open up Firefox, right
click the menu bar and uncheck the **Menu Bar** item. Then, go to the
Firefox menu and access the **Add-ons manager**.

The add-ons we will use are:

• Movable Firefox Button

• Ad-block Plus

Install both by searching for them in the search box, and then restart
as required.

Next, we will do some coding with XUL and Javascript.

29.3. Creating our add-on

Firefox add-ons are easy to build and can be used without the need to upload them to the Mozilla website. We will create an add-on to create a clock button, and to control the behavior of Firefox on the screen every time it loads.

29.3.1. Folder and file structure

Start by creating the files and folders:

```
$ cd ~/.mozilla/firefox/kiosk.default/extensions
$ mkdir -p clock@kiosk.com/chrome
$ cd clock@kiosk.com
$ touch install.rdf chrome.manifest
$ cd chrome
$ touch clock.xul clock.js clock.css
```

The resulting file structure will look like this:

```
clock@kiosk.com/
        chrome.manifest
        install.rdf
        chrome/
                clock.css
                clock.js
                clock.xul
```

The manifest and the rdf files will set up our add-on to be viewed and loaded by Firefox. The chrome directory (which doesn't have anything to do with Google Chrome or Chromium browser) will hold the add-on files. Edit each of them with its contents:

chrome.manifest

```
content clock chrome/

# long line
style chrome://global/content/customizeToolbar.xul \
chrome://clock/content/clock.css
# another long line
overlay chrome://browser/content/browser.xul \
chrome://clock/content/clock.xul
```

Please note the line continuations - this is not a shell script, so the long lines will need to be intact. Remove the \ line continuation sign, and put the following line on the same line.

install.rdf

```
<?xml version="1.0"?>

<RDF
  xmlns="http://www.w3.org/1999/02/22-rdf-syntax-ns#"
  xmlns:em="http://www.mozilla.org/2004/em-rdf#">

  <Description
      about="urn:mozilla:install-manifest"

      em:name="clock"
      em:description="Clock for Kiosk"
      em:creator="Zendrael"

      em:id="clock@kiosk.com"
      em:version="1.0"
      em:homepageURL="http://www.zendrael.com/kiosk"

      em:iconURL="chrome://clock/content/icon.png">

      <em:targetApplication><!-- Firefox -->
      <Description
      em:id="{ec8030f7-c20a-464f-9b0e-13a3a9e97384}"
      em:minVersion="5.0"
      em:maxVersion="99" />
      </em:targetApplication>

      <em:file>
      <Description
      about="urn:mozilla:extension:clock"
      em:package="content/clock/" />
      </em:file>
  </Description>
</RDF>
```

chrome/clock.css

```css
/* let the buttons be smaller */
.clean {
    padding: 0px;
    margin: 0px;
}

/* remove arrow from buttons */
.clean .toolbarbutton-menu-dropmarker {
    display: none !important;
}

#osStatus-button-clock {
    padding-top: 5px;
    margin-right: 3px;
}

#appmenu-toolbar-button
  .toolbarbutton-menu-dropmarker {
    display: none !important;
}

toolbar:not([mode="text"]) #appmenu-toolbar-button
  > .toolbarbutton-icon,
toolbar:not([mode="text"]) #appmenu-button
  > .button-box .button-icon {
    list-style-image:
      url("moz-icon://stock/system-run?size=16")
      !important;
}

toolbar[mode="icons"] #appmenu-toolbar-button
  > .toolbarbutton-text,
toolbar[mode="icons"] #appmenu-button
  > .button-box .button-text {
    display: none;
}
```

chrome/clock.js

```javascript
// Start main window without borders
// Note the long line
document.getElementById("main-window").\
  setAttribute("hidechrome","true");

/*
    function clock
        show the time and date
*/
function getClock(){
    var obj = \
        document.getElementById("osStatus-button-clock");

    var now = new Date();
    var hours = now.getHours();
    var minutes = now.getMinutes();
    var seconds = now.getSeconds();
    var timeValue = ""+ hours;

    timeValue +=
        ((minutes<10) ? ":0" : ":") + minutes;

    //set date
    var month = now.getMonth() + 1;
    var day = now.getDate();
    var year = now.getFullYear();
    var dateValue = day + "/" + month + "/" + year;

    obj.setAttribute("value", timeValue);
    obj.setAttribute("tooltiptext", dateValue);
}

//set timeout events, updating clock
setInterval( "getClock()", 1000 );
```

chrome/clock.xul

```xml
<?xml version="1.0" encoding="UTF-8"?>
<?xml-stylesheet type="text/css"
  href="chrome://clock/content/clock.css"?>

<!DOCTYPE overlay >
<overlay id="custombutton-overlay"
  xmlns="http://www.mozilla.org/keymaster/ \
    gatekeeper/there.is.only.xul">

<script type="application/javascript"
  src="chrome://clock/content/clock.js"/>

<!-- Firefox -->
<toolbarpalette id="BrowserToolbarPalette">
  <toolbaritem id="osStatusItems"
    label="OS Status Items">
    <label id="osStatus-button-clock"/>
  </toolbaritem>
</toolbarpalette>

<!-- button details -->
<label id="osStatus-button-clock"
  value="00:00"
  tooltiptext="00/00/0000"
  class="toolbarbutton-1 \
    chromeclass-toolbar-additional clean"
  crop="none" orient="horizontal" dir="reverse"
  />

</overlay>
```

Note the two line continuations here too - the mozilla.org link needs
to be without spaces.

Now, start Firefox. It may ask if you want to install our clock
extension: do so.

After a restart, nothing will change; we need to right-click the toolbar and go to **Customize**. In the window we will find our clock add-on. Drag it to the right side of the + button in the same bar that tabs appear.

Restart and close Firefox once more.

29.4. Shutdown considerations

It's desirable to be able to turn off our system by the power switch, making the kiosk more reliable in the event of power loss.

To do this, enable **copy2fs** via the **Toggle default install to file system** option in **Apps**. Now all extensions are loaded to RAM.

As the final step, we will unmount the disk after the boot has completed. This will prevent any corruption from getting to the disk, enabling clean shutdowns via the power switch.

Add the following to **/opt/bootlocal.sh**, replacing **sda1** with your drive:

```
umount /mnt/sda1
```

29.5. Results

Turning this from a HD-based install to a PXE-based one would let you have an easily managed fleet of diskless web kiosks.

Reboot the system and you will get Firefox taking all the desktop without the title bar and with the clock working. Our kiosk is now ready!

At the time of writing, the Firefox version was 21. The install used about 54 Mb of space. When just started, displaying the default Firefox homepage, the RAM usage was 232 Mb.

The exact requirements depend on the web pages you intend to allow, but 256 Mb would be tight. 512 Mb of RAM would be recommended for this use.

Index

Lightning Source UK Ltd.
Milton Keynes UK
UKOW04f1811220615

253939UK00001B/108/P